AUSCHWITZ ESCAPE

The Klara Wizel Story

by

Danny Naten and R. J. Gifford

Compiled and published by Beverly Naten

ISBN: 1502416395
ISBN 13: 978-1502416391
Library of Congress Control Number: 2014920501
CreateSpace Independent Publishing Platform,
North Charleston, South Carolina
Copyright Registration Number: TXu 1-825-731

*This book is dedicated to Klara and Beverly,
the strongest women I know. Their courage and their
heart can teach anyone touched by great loss, whether it
be the loss of a generation or the loss of only one person
who was held so dear.*

CHAPTERS

Prologue..1

The Early Years 7

Hitler Watch / Moralizing Anti-Semitism 19

Legalizing Anti-Semitism....................................23

Slipping into Darkness / The Last Match.................29

Kill Boxes 33

Sighet and the German Occupation 35

Legalized Theft 39

Serpent Street / The Sighet Ghetto 47

Deportation / The Nazi Deceit...............................51

Dr. Josef Mengele / The Murderer in White............63

Auschwitz-Birkenau The Final Solution / A Syllabus of Death 67

The Demoralization Process 75

Life and Death at Auschwitz 81

Hedy and Rose...95

Separated from Rose 101

Selected by Dr. Josef Mengele.................. 103

My Escape... 111

Humanity.. 123

Mengele on the Run 133

The Journey Home................................. 135

The Search Begins................................. 147

Going to Prague.................................... 151

A Whole New Chapter 157

The World Gets Bigger 165

Epilogue... 175

Afterword 191

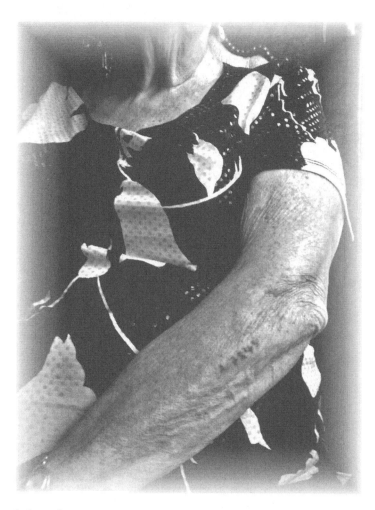

And then the tattoo...Numbers were painfully inked onto our arms.
Mine was A-7845. This was the Nazis' way of permanently dehuman-
izing us especially for traditional Jewish families like ours where tat-
tooing is prohibited.

AUSCHWITZ ESCAPE

The Klara Wizel Story

by

Danny Naten and R. J. Gifford

Compiled and published by Beverly Naten

PROLOGUE

In 1933, former General Erich Ludendorff sent a telegram to President Hindenburg regarding the appointment of his new chancellor, Adolf Hitler.

> By appointing Adolf Hitler Chancellor of the Reich, you have handed over our sacred German fatherland to one of the greatest demagogues of all time. I prophesy to you this evil man will plunge our Reich into the abyss and will inflict immeasurable woe on our nation. Future generations will curse you in your grave for this action.[1]

Although Hans Frank, who served as Reichsminister and general governor of Poland during the Nazi era, claimed to have read it, an original copy of the telegram has never been found. Hans Frank wrote about the document in his memoirs just before his execution as a war criminal. Another source, which was considered to be more reliable, was Captain Wilhelm Breuker, a close associate of Ludendorff. When Breuker wrote his memoirs in 1953, like Hans Frank, he also attested to the existence of the telegram.

The concern that the telegram ever existed has caused great debate among the collective competitive insiders, historians, academics, political war buffs, and media. Whether or not the telegram ever existed can be argued until the end of time. The clear message it contains and the insight that it reveals provides for humankind such an ingenious historical forecast. We chose to place it, in all its glory, at the prologue and state that the text, real or not real, is one of the most powerful and straightforward statements ever written about Adolf Hitler.

With our introduction of the Ludendorff telegram, not much more has to be said of Hitler's character. Millions of words have been written about Hitler, as I'm sure many millions more will be written. There are more than thirty-two thousand books with his name in the title. Much more important is the effect his action had on Klara's family, millions of other families like hers, and the rest of the world. Klara and her family experienced the beginning of Hitler's rise to power in Germany all the way through the crushing end of World War II in Europe on May 4, 1945.

January 30, 1933, the day Hitler was appointed chancellor of Germany, and what followed in an eight-year span, altered the world so radically that Germany and the world are still re-covering. World War II was the deadliest military conflict in history. This widespread war, which so thoroughly engulfed the planet, involved sixty-one countries. The line between civilians and military became increasingly blurred, and not a single person was unaffected. Hitler's war machine would force an enormous global calling of all human, economic, industrial, and scientific resources to defeat his empire. World War II is estimated to have caused fifty to seventy million deaths, all of which are the responsibility of one man: Adolf Hitler.

It's been determined by some that the average person meets approximately sixty to one hundred thousand people in his or her lifetime. Although there are several possible ways of calculating this number, it could be more, or it could be less. The majority of these meetings are brief, customary name exchanges. Usually they include a hello, a short, quick handshake, and a farewell. Personality, status, profession, and geographical location all play a huge role in how many people the average person meets in a typical life-span. Only a very small percentage of those interactions result in any real, consequential long-term relationships. No matter how brief, what all encounters do provide are opportunity. People meeting people makes the world go round.

Nowhere in modern history has any one man had more of a unique opportunity to meet thousands and thousands of people face-to-face on a daily basis, do his duty, be humane, save lives, and apply the wisdom and values of the Hippocratic oath than Dr. Josef Mengele. Despite this, Josef Mengele was recruited to implement Hitler's fanatical genocidal policies against Jews and other races at Auschwitz-Birkenau. Given authority as an SS representative, Mengele abandoned his sworn humanitarian oath as a doctor. He enthusiastically chose to replace good with evil. Extremely ambitious, Mengele rededicated his allegiance to Hitler by joining the SS and taking the sacred oath, pledging his obedience to Adolf Hitler.

All eyewitness accounts state that he was unquestionably not an average man. His smile and outstretched arms appeared angel-like as he stood wearing his lab coat that glowed in the light. Known as the Angel of Death, Mengele conducted business at Auschwitz like a wolf in sheep's clothing as he personally met and sent more than four hundred thousand people to their deaths.

Mengele, a collaborator in Hitler's massive war crimes, exploited his humanitarian obligation. Mengele and Hitler left in their wake a legacy so morally corrupt that their actions still shatter the heart some sixty years later. Mengele misrepresented a unique opportunity to serve. Instead, he attempted to completely wipe out a whole segment of society: the Jews.

Klara's story is a love story. It's essential that you travel her road. Under Nazi tyranny with millions of other people, this brave young girl takes a miraculous journey from the edge of death at Auschwitz-Birkenau to a new life after the war. At seventeen years old, Klara Iutkovits questions life, surrenders to death, and challenges the human spirit every step of her way. No way of knowing then that her guiltless encounters with the creature Dr. Josef Mengele would make her an eternal part of the notorious Nazi legend, Klara's story defies the odds as it is a battle to explain the unexplainable.

This is Klara's story.

THE EARLY YEARS

On January 15, 1927, Klara was born in Sighet, Transylvania. Belonging to the Kingdom of Greater Romania, Transylvania was then the regional capital. At that time, Sighet was a small town of twenty-eight thousand in northern Romania near where the Hungarian and Ukrainian borders met. In 1927 and during World War II, Sighet was mostly a Jewish community. For its time and size, it was very modern and reasonably successful. Full of life, with a very active community, Sighet's free-market society had movie theaters, shops, schools, markets, synagogues, import and export businesses, doctors, and businessmen. Klara attended school in Sighet with her brothers and sisters. Her life revolved around her large Jewish family.

Sighet, Romania, Hungary, the war, the Holocaust. What would you like to know? I come from a very, very nice, loving family. We were ten children—five boys and five girls—and my parents. Most children would say they had the best parents, but mine really were. I was a very happy child. All of us were very happy because it was a very nice, close family.

I was thirteen years old when I first saw a uniformed German soldier walking the streets of my hometown. This is not the beginning of my story, but it is a good starting place. The uniform was green. I bet the Germans spent a lot of time thinking about how good an army marching in all green would look on the battlefield, and how it might blend into the world around it when the fighting stopped. How nice the young men would look, so nice that others would look up to them and want to join them. Even after all that happened to me, I did not mind the green uniforms and did not fear them. I even sometimes liked the people who wore them, but that is coming soon, so I will not spoil it.

There were twelve of us in my beautiful family. I know how that sounds today, but large families were common at that time in Sighet. My parents were Ignatiu and Freda Iutkovits. My brothers, in order from oldest to youngest, were Joseph, Lazar, Haskell, Mendal, and Mortho. And my sisters were Ety, Ancy, Rose, and Hedy. And then there was me, Klara. I was the youngest daughter.

Our business was a family affair. My mother, Freda, ran the daily business with my oldest brother, Joseph. We were a distributor to local businesses. We sold dry goods: cooking oil, flour, and any of the necessary items of the day. Because my mother did not always have a lot of free time, I would often prepare and bring her lunch.

It was my brother's job to travel and buy the products from neighboring cities. He traveled weeks at a time, so we didn't get to see him very much. When Joseph would return home, he would always gratify us with these wonderful stories about his journeys and special gifts he would pick from the different countries he would visit. It was always a fun celebration. He was a great businessman and a dedicated son committed to providing the rest of his family with a comfortable life.

Klara's oldest brother Joseph with friends, before the war. Joseph is on the right.

Because my mother and Joseph were very successful in our business, we were able to afford a nice home with five bedrooms. We had two maids who helped around the house, and an older woman who cooked for us. Our table was always full, and there was always plenty of family around it.

Under my father's leadership, we were always encouraged to be generous individuals. My brothers were all handsome, kind, and outgoing. My sisters were all energetic, very beautiful, loving, and smart.

My father was traditional. He was a holy man, a scholar who loved to study the Torah. He was also so kind and so decent that even his most serious tone would make me smile on the inside and know that even his harshest words would eventually balance out in the end.

My father was a very loving man, and he was probably the first to die, so I want to keep him in my account for as long as possible. He kept a close eye on me, probably because of my rebellious nature, and life's lessons were more valuable than gold to him. He was always ready for an opportunity to teach or pass on wisdom. There were plenty of us to provide him with that opportunity. He taught me a great deal about humanity and my obligation to be true to myself and others. Like most lessons, we learn from our weaknesses if we have the right mentor, like my father, to guide us.

Let me start by saying, I used to love the movies, and when I was ten years old, I started going to the movies with my girlfriend Sara, who was my best friend at the time. Sara and I loved going to the movies together, and there were two theaters in our town. Sara lived close by, and on the weekends, free from school, we would often walk through town to get there. I knew every seat in each of the movie houses, and we saw movies from Sweden, Hungary, and America. My favorites were always the American movies. I believe it would have cost about fifty cents in US currency to get in, but we paid with Hungarian currency, called pengö. There was nothing special about the buildings, but they were nonetheless magical. In a way, they were my first glimpse at my future.

Sara and I were fortunate enough, back then, to have seen *Gone with the Wind* when it first came to Sighet. You can imagine how excited we must have been going to see the great American star Clark Gable. To us, our small-town theaters were as bright and beautiful as any place on Earth. The stories in the movies we saw were hopelessly romantic, and many of them were endlessly optimistic.

My father had only one condition about going to the movies. We were not supposed to attend them on the Sabbath. Since Sighet was mainly Jewish, all of the Jewish businesses were closed on the Sabbath except the two movie theaters, which provided entertainment. You have to understand, I was more rebellious than any of my brothers and sisters, and Sara and I wanted to do what we wanted to do, and we did it. There was no problem until one day, as we were leaving the theater, we saw a friend of my father's coming out of the synagogue. I was not sure if he had seen me, or at least, that is what I said to my friend, but I remember feeling a bit panicky about it. I rehearsed in my mind what I would say if my father asked.

When I got home, my father called me into his study. He had just been on the phone with his friend, who told him he saw me coming out of the movie theater. I had always been proud of the fact that we had a telephone in our house because it was so rare to have a phone back then. But honestly, at that moment, I wished we did not have one.

He said, "Klara, have you been to the movies on the Sabbath?"

I told him that it was impossible, that I hadn't been there, and that there was no possibility that I was lying. I remember he looked at me for a long time. I thought he was punishing me with his silence.

Then he said, "Klara, I really want you to listen to what I'm about to say next." He told me that he believed me and that he would always believe me. Then he reminded me that Saturday was not a day for movies; it was for God. He smiled and told me that he would never remind me again.

I left, never forgetting how much he loved and trusted me. I never went to the movies on the Sabbath again. I felt so strange and relieved, yet understood at the same time. Being young, I bounced back pretty quickly because for my friends and me, it was a wonderful and carefree time.

Back then in Europe, men really treated a girl, or a lady, how a lady should be treated: with great respect and honor. The men would always open the door for you, or they would say hello to you as they passed by. Most men wore caps or bowler hats, even in the summertime. When they greeted you, they would say, "I kiss your hand," and they would take off their hats and say hello to you. They honored you because you were a lady and for no other reason except that you were a lady. It was in my opinion that this was the way a lady should be treated all the time, like that, absolutely!

My trips to town were always fun, and that's where I learned a lot about life and people. Of course, there were different stores to window-shop in, and my friends and I would never forget to stop at a bakery called Stein's. All they made there were different kinds of cakes, no bread or any other bakery items, just cakes. My favorite was a special rum-type cake that was so delicious I can still taste it today. On our way home, my friends and I would pass by a beautiful park in the center of town with large oak and maple trees that covered the grounds. A lot of, mostly young, men would gather there to watch these very fashionably dressed women parade by on their daily walk, which was always a big social event. My favorite time of year to go was when it snowed because it always seemed so romantic to me.

School wasn't really my favorite place to be, and at the time, I failed to recognize the benefit and value of that privilege. But I did learn to read pretty quickly and devoured everything in sight from French author Émile Zola, Polish writer Sholem Asch, to various Hungarian authors, and of course, Margaret Mitchell, who wrote *Gone with the Wind*. Our home had a beautiful garden where I could go and read, and I would get lost for hours in one of those wonderful books.

Shabbat was always a very special time for my family and me. It is a Jewish tradition and ritual that starts every Friday at sundown and ends Saturday evening. It is primarily a day of rest and spiritual enrichment. Shabbat remains so joyous a memory because the twelve of us were all together as a complete family. We all had different duties in the preparation. Actually, the preparation really started on Thursday, because we were such a big family. Irina was one of our maids, whom I loved dearly and who survived the war. She prepared the challah. I still remember her getting the white flour dough ready to bake, rolling it into a rope shape, and brushing it with an egg wash that would always give it that glossy look. The smell of the bread baking in the oven and watching Irina with her routine and her chores always made me feel safe and secure. She was always considered one of the family and was a dear friend to me. Many times, my older sister Rose, would bring the fish from the market, usually carp, as everybody helped a little bit. Joseph, my oldest brother, would say a prayer for the wine, and we would drink a little, and then he would say a prayer for the bread. When Joseph was on a business trip and could not be at Shabbat with us, Lazar would say the prayers. Haskell, Mendal, and Mortho, my youngest brother, would sit next to my father and help with cleanup, as we all did. We had twelve beautiful silver candelabras that represented each one of us and were lit every week. Those candelabras would later be confiscated by the pro-Nazi Hungarian government. My sister Hedy was in charge of bringing the dessert plates to the table, which had apples, prunes, and assorted fruits. She also gathered the dessert plates, when finished, and took them back to the kitchen. Hedy loved the juice from the dessert and would dip a piece of the leftover challah into the juice, which was flavored with lemon and a little bit of sugar and vanilla. Needless to say, this quickly became her favorite job.

My mother would pass around the matzo ball soup, starting with the oldest and then to the youngest. I was not a real big fan of the soup, but I ate it out of love for my mother.

A driver of a horse and buggy would bring seltzer to our home during the middle of the week, but sometimes he wouldn't come, so I would go to the store to get two bottles of seltzer and bring it to our home. It all seems chaotic when I think about it now, but really, our family's observance of Shabbat meals was very formal and very neat, served in a very elegant way.

Of course, there was traditional song, and my father would always start the singing. There were twelve of us, and we sounded like a choir. It was a very happy time.

We celebrated all of the Jewish holidays, Hanukkah, Pesach (Passover), Yom Kippur, as did our community. We would always bake cakes for one another and give them to our friends as they would to us. Irina would deliver the cakes, and the people would tip her. Sometimes, she needed my help in finding where the people lived, so I was happy to show her, but in return, I would ask for a part of her tips, and she would give it to me. I was maybe ten years old at the time, and I laugh about it now. Nobody ever gave material gifts, just homemade cakes, all made with love. My sister Ety usually baked our cakes. Oranges were a novelty, as we couldn't grow them because the weather didn't allow for it, so they were mostly imported from the United States. Sometimes we included them with the cakes.

My father instilled a very strong sense of giving in all of us from a very early age. Our business did very well, so for me, it was second nature to help those in need. In Sighet, Wednesday was the day chosen for people who were poor to come to the different stores for help. My mother nominated me to give out money and food donations to people who needed aid and support. I found out from different people in town that we always gave the most. My father, of course, demanded it, which didn't always go over well with my mother. She often found out after the fact that he had given away more than they had budgeted. People were always very grateful and showed their gratitude by giving my family their blessing. I looked forward to this weekly ritual, because it taught me responsibility toward people who were less fortunate. My father knew he could count on me to help him with something that was extremely important to him.

My sister Ancy had a Chinese armoire full of dresses and was very into fashion. She had a great figure and seemed to always be at the dressmaker. I remember Ancy would always dress very elegantly.

She made me laugh because when she opened her armoire, even though it was full of beautiful dresses, she would say, "Look, Klara, I have nothing to wear!"

I was the ninth. My oldest sister, Ety, practically raised me and my younger brother, Mortho. I still remember when I was nine years old, being at her wedding and not being able to stop crying. I didn't want her to leave our home. It was like losing my mother. I remember in the summer, when I didn't go to school, she would come and get me and take me everywhere with her. I felt I was losing my sister and my best friend at the same time. All of those tears were for nothing, but how can you tell a little girl that and make her believe?

Our neighbors were mostly Jewish. However, one family that lived a couple of houses down were Hungarian. I would play with one of their daughters when I was young, and she would appear in my life on and off. As we got older, we drifted apart because our interests grew quite different, but there was a moment with her that I will write about later that has affected me to this day.

HITLER WATCH/
MORALIZING ANTI-SEMITISM

At the time of Hitler's rise to power, Germany lay encircled by ten separate countries: Austria, Czechoslovakia, Poland, Sweden, Denmark, The Netherlands, Belgium, France, Switzerland, and Italy. Hitler considered these countries rivals and an ideological and military threat to his agenda. He wanted the unification of these countries to create a powerful economic and military force that would serve Germany. Hitler wanted Europe under German control. He believed occupying, securing financial takeover, and changing the political landscape of these countries were the keys to his success. World War I had left Germany in dire straits financially, and by 1921, the country was confronting massive unemployment, skyrocketing inflation, and the brink of civil war. Germany was rapidly sinking into the abyss, desperate to survive and reinvent itself. Now more than ever, it was in need of strong headship and direction.

With all the conditions being right, and having been on the scene since 1921, Hitler would make his move to become the absolute, undisputable leader of an extremely vulnerable German nation. Now a cunning and powerful leader, with an uncompromising, fierce ability to articulate and inflame large crowds, Hitler became that dark star to take control. Seizing the opportunity, he hypnotized Germany with his charismatic speeches and powerful propaganda, commanding citizens to surrender to him and him only. Adolf Hitler was voted in and confirmed as the Führer, the new leader of the National Social Workers Party in 1921.

In 1923, directed by Hitler, the party attempted a coup on the German government at a large open assembly. The assembly was held at the Bürgerbräukeller in Munich, Germany, and became what is now known as the infamous Beer Hall Putsch. There, Hitler and an armed militia attempted to take over the local military but were put down by the district police. Sixteen of Hitler's followers were killed, and Hitler was arrested. Hitler was placed on trial which he used to spread his propaganda. He was sentenced to prison, where he quickly became a hero.

Written in 1925, while Hitler was in prison for the Beer Hall Putsch, *Mein Kampf* (*My Battle*) was an autobiography and description of Hitler's fanatical ideology. The book was Hitler's vow of indifference to Jews and the rest of the world, inundated throughout with intense anti-Semitism. From

Hitler's twisted perception, Jews were responsible for the existence of everything wicked, and he wanted Germany to embrace his evil ideas. In *Mein Kampf,* Hitler gave birth to his fanatical Aryan ideology and his desire to eliminate the European Jew by moralizing anti-Semitism. Hitler made "the Jewish question" a moral dilemma, and any German citizen who did not agree with his views would be considered morally corrupt. In *Mein Kampf,* Hitler aggressively plotted a step-by-step movement to conquer Europe and ultimately dominate the world.

By 1929, the Great Depression had hit. Germany had become dependent on short-term loans from the United States that were vital to its economy. One by one, the loans were called in, and by 1932, the unemployment rate had risen to an astounding 29.9 percent.

Now it was in writing for all to see. The fact that millions of people would listen to and follow him would disgracefully legitimize Hitler and his evil ideology by giving more power to his obsession, making him a millionaire, a national figure in Germany, and the most dangerous man in the world.

LEGALIZING ANTI-SEMITISM

Although the world's governments watched Hitler's rise to power, and the Nazification of Germany, the majority of citizens of the surrounding countries, including young Klara and her family, held the outlook that it was something happening far off and was not of major concern. People were afraid, nevertheless.

Most felt it would never affect them because, as Klara would say, "I was very young, and we really didn't talk about it much...After all, it was isolated in Germany. However, I realize now, we should have listened more. Although we felt safe in Sighet, we were well aware of the Jewish stores in Germany that were picketed, and shop owners of these stores were beaten and harassed. It was not something that was often discussed openly in our community. Although, being Jewish, we felt the intimidation all the way from Germany but kept quiet and went about our daily lives."

Hitler, however fanatical, did have opposition. In March of 1933, in New York City, ten thousand Jewish former soldiers marched to city hall to hold protest demonstrations against the treatment of Jews in Germany. Comparable protests were held at Madison Square Garden, where fifty-five thousand people attended. In Boston, Baltimore, Cleveland, and many other locations in the United States, consumers boycotted the sale of German goods. The protests were broadcast worldwide. Concurrently, the headline "Judea Declares War on Germany, Jews of All the World Unite" appeared on the front page of London's *Daily Express*.

As some feared, the Nazis threatened to retaliate if these protests continued. Jews were trapped in Germany, unarmed and unable to fight back against Hitler's club-wielding Brown Shirt police. Their stores were picketed by thugs. Shoppers at these stores were intimidated and harassed with no recourse. Joseph Goebbels, Germany's notorious propaganda minister, and Hermann Göring, head of the German state police, held a one-day boycott of Jewish business. Goebbels claimed the German boycott would destroy Germany's economy.

In addition, Goebbels would claim the Nazis' stance. He let everybody know, "If worldwide Jewish attacks on the Nazi regime continue, the boycott will be resumed until German Jewry has been annihilated."[2]

Göring also gave notice. He said that he would also use the police and very strongly. He refused the thought that they were only protectors for Jewish stores but to protect anyone who comes into Germany but in no way was their purpose to protect the Jewish usurers.

All Jews were now considered subversive enemy agents by the Nazi regime. The leaders of the Jewish protest took a vote and called off any further demonstration. They feared the rallying would cause much more serious treatment of the Jews of Germany; little did they know it was too late. It would pale in comparison with what was about to come, and the Nazis' enormous atrocities aimed at the Jews in Europe would not be exposed for twelve long years.

In 1933, no one could have imagined that within seven years, Hitler would occupy, control, and have direct authority of Germany's ten surrounding countries. And after only three months in his position as chancellor of Germany, Hitler began his campaign to eliminate the Jews from Germany and Europe. All media, literature, music, newspapers, and public events were censored and directly controlled by the state and Joseph Goebbels. Goebbels's propaganda machine was in full force as the hatred Hitler intended for Jews intensified in Germany. Countless shop and restaurant owners across Germany took it upon themselves to boycott Jewish businesses and refused to serve the Jewish population. Signs stating "Jews not admitted" and "Jews enter this place at their own risk" appeared all over Germany.

While the anti-Semitism firestorm swept across Germany, many Jewish people left the country. Celebrated Jews like Albert Einstein and others reluctantly abandoned their residences in Germany and immigrated to Great Britain and other countries in Europe. In 1935, Hitler legalized anti-Semitism by passing the Nuremberg Laws on Citizenship and Race. These laws stripped Jews of their citizenship and made it illegal to marry Aryans. As pressure mounted, *Mein Kampf* was given freely to newlywed couples and every German soldier.

Conspiring to step up the emigration of the Jews in 1938, the Nazis created Kristallnacht, or "Night of Broken Glass," a government persecution of Jews in Germany, Austria, and Sudeten, a region of Czechoslovakia. Hitler used an incident involving a German diplomat who worked for the German Embassy in Paris. He had been murdered by Herschel Grynszpan, a furious young Jewish refugee, after he learned his parents had been deported back to Poland. Under Hitler's command, the German hierarchy inflamed the incident. The Nazis used it to enrage German citizens by dispatching the state-controlled media outlets. Using the incident and the new Nuremberg Laws on Citizenship and Race, Herman Göring unleashed the state police while encouraging German citizens toward violence against Jews and Jewish establishments. During Kristallnacht, more than 7,500 Jewish shops were destroyed, and four hundred synagogues were burned. Ninety-one Jews were killed. Hitler had already established camps for political prisoners. Now, and for the first time, an estimated twenty thousand Jews were sent to concentration camps. Kristallnacht was the catalyst that caused Jews throughout all of Europe to want to flee and escape the Nazi suppression and go anywhere that was considered safe. After

Kristallnacht, between 1935 and 1939, approx
Jewish population of Germany fled the countr

———∞∞∞———

Kristallnacht was a big turning point for our town and for all
of the Jews in Europe. Although we lived in Transylvania,
people fled from the Nazis through Czechoslovakia and came
to our town, Sighet, for help. Men, women, and children were
crying. People were very upset because they had lost their
homes and possessions. Our family helped with food, shelter,
and clothing; everybody pitched in and gave something. I
was so young, but we realized very quickly that Hitler's plan,
his conspiracy, was creeping our way. His objective was to
make it so uncomfortable for the Jews in Germany that the
people would leave their homes and migrate elsewhere.
Of course, little did we know that it was his plan for us and
the rest of Europe, and *that* plan was only what you could
see on the surface. Underneath was something waiting for
us that no human being could ever imagine. We just never
thought it would arrive in Romania. You just don't think that
way. We should have, but we just didn't. In 1939, when I was
thirteen years old, Hitler's master plan for the world would be
unwrapped for everyone to see. From that point on, the world
as we knew it would be changed forever.

SLIPPING INTO DARKNESS / THE LAST MATCH

On Sunday, August 27, 1939, Poland played Hungary in an international soccer match at Wojska Polskiego Stadium in Warsaw, Poland. Considered one of the best teams in the world, Hungary was expected to easily win and had beaten Poland nine times; the Poles had never won against Hungary before. The largest Polish national newspaper sports headline read, "Without Chance but Ready to Fight."

The game started out with Hungary pulling ahead 2–0 in the first thirty minutes. Shortly after, Poland's best player, a forward named Ernest Wilimowski, scored the team's first goal. In the second half, Poland attacked with focus and fierceness and scored its second goal, which sent the crowd into an uproar. From that point on, it seemed that the whole game shifted in Poland's favor. When the game ended, Poland had beaten the heavily favored Hungary 4–2.

Polish Colonel Kazimierz Glabisz mentioned during the after-game banquet that this may be the last game before another war.

Little did he know how prophetic his statement would be. Four days before the game, Germany and the Soviet Union had finalized a plan and secretly put into motion an organized invasion into Poland. Five days later, on September 1, 1939, Germany invaded Poland and started World War II. Sixteen days later, the Soviet Union attacked Eastern Poland. Stalin and Hitler decided to divide up Poland between the two countries.

My brother Lazar, he was a very good soccer player and loved the Hungarian national team. He knew all the players' names by heart. Of course, I was always happy for him when we won, but being a girl back home in 1939, well, I just didn't have the heart to tell him I really didn't care that much. Girls were just not interested in sports like soccer back then. But all my brothers were; they loved soccer, skiing, bike riding, and mountain climbing. They were all pretty outgoing.

Growing up, all we had at the time was a radio; there was no TV. I remember being huddled around the radio with my family and listening to the news reports. There was an atmosphere of terrible fear and sadness in my home, and in Sighet, after Hitler invaded Poland. Maybe you can understand how this last soccer match became very meaningful to us all.

KILL BOXES

In November, the first Jewish ghetto was established in Piotrków, Poland. In 1942, the infamous Wannsee Conference was held and set in motion the Final Solution. The Wannsee Conference was a highly secure meeting that was attended by fourteen high-ranking German officers. There, the fate of the European Jew would be decided.

The Jewish ghettos came first and were proudly referred to as "kill boxes" by the Nazi propaganda minister Joseph Goebbels. The Jewish ghetto was an extremely sophisticated plot, developed and implemented by Hitler's top SS leaders. Jewish ghettos were created and designed to expand across Europe, and over a period of time, they were perfected. The operation was an ongoing roundup and detention of Jews across Europe. By law, Jews were forced to leave their homes and all their possessions and were forced to live in isolated areas away from the main population, restricted by high walls and wire fences. Ghettos emerged all over Poland, and Jews were forced at gunpoint to live in crowded, unsanitary conditions. They were not allowed to leave except in special situations. Any Jew caught outside the ghetto without permission could be executed on sight.

The Warsaw ghetto was the largest in Poland, with a population of 380,000 people. The highly classified, cryptic complexities developed at the Wannsee Conference would grow and advance, taking on new life with an almost supernatural momentum. This Jewish ghetto would inevitably cross an invisible line of no return and plunge Jews, the German people, and the world into an abyss so dark that when it was all over, the world would be forced to live with this mortal wound for generations to come. In May 1940, the Auschwitz concentration camp was established near the Polish city of Oświęcim.

SIGHET AND THE GERMAN OCCUPATION

In 1940, the Hungarian king signed a treaty that gave the Nazis the right to make and enforce their own authority within Hungarian borders. The northern half of Transylvania was annexed to Hungary during the Second World War. Sighet would now be occupied and controlled by the Nazis. We looked at it the way a rail views an oncoming train. There was a trembling at the thought of what was to come, a certain shiver of fear, but there was nothing to be done about it. You could only wish that the train would stay far away, because when it came closer, it would be at full force.

My last year of school was when I was thirteen years old. I was walking home from school the first time I saw a German soldier. I usually walked home with Rose or a friend. German soldiers weren't common, and I didn't want to get caught staring at them. They were from another world. They didn't bother us, and we didn't bother them. Of course, there was tension, especially after the Germans came into Sighet. Although the German soldiers didn't disrespect us, their presence seemed to embolden the Hungarian soldiers. The words the Hungarian soldiers and police would call us in passing, I'd rather not repeat. My father would never approve of those kinds of words, even if I only said them in my head, much less out loud.

The German soldier I saw that day, wearing a green uniform, passed by me and was gone. The next day, there were probably two German soldiers on the street. Then there were four. Finally, there were enough that they traveled in large groups. Their presence was menacing enough; they were the powerful German army—the occupiers. They commanded the anti-Semitic Hungarian army and police to carry out their orders. The Hungarians were happy to do it. The SS, the ones dressed in black, were a different story. I observed a few of them walking around, but more would follow. I rarely saw them.

One day, we got a visit from the German military. My mother and father were told that we would be having a German officer as a houseguest for a few weeks and to prepare a room. There was no objecting to the decision; we just did what we were told and hoped for the best. Fortunately, this time, the officer who came to live with us was a captain in the German army. My family came to enjoy his company. My mother spoke very good German, and the officer was impressed. He spent time with us, and upon hearing that he was leaving, my father invited him to our family dinner. This was a great honor. He sat beside my father as a welcomed guest. He kissed my mother's hand. It was the last civilized gesture I would see from a man in uniform for quite some time. There were tears when he left. Of course, soon, there would be tears so natural that they were almost like breathing. But, of course, we did not know this then.

LEGALIZED THEFT

It wasn't too long after the German captain left that our conditions began to rapidly deteriorate. We were told to give away whatever gold or silver we had to the government. Since Sighet was not a very big town, it was easy for the SS to locate the wealthier families, the people who had something of value to take away. The anti-Semitic Hungarian army and police were enforcing the SS's policies. I'll never forget the day the chief of police came into our home with a small team and took away anything that we owned that was made of gold or silver. We didn't give them everything, though. We hid some things in the floorboards of the house. Later, they returned and accused us of lying and not giving them everything we had, so they took my brother Mendal and arrested him. They took him down to the police station and interrogated him. They repeatedly struck him across the face, and shouted at him, "Tell us where you hid the stuff!" But he wouldn't talk. Mendal never told them where it was.

Our clampdown began slowly and with a hidden hostility, but things quickly began to escalate. First, they closed the school to Jews, but everyone else was allowed to go. My sister Rose got angry. She stayed even after she was told to go home. The teacher threatened Rose, and we pulled at her dress and made her come with us. This teacher was supposed to be the educator, and yet all she could pass on was a dislike for my kind. It seemed strange how an educated person convinced herself of the purity of her own thoughts, even when they made no sense.

"You are an educator. Are you educating by sending us home?"

This kind of thought was not sophisticated enough for her, I guess. We went home. That was my last day in school. Jews were no longer allowed there. We stayed home. Jews were no longer allowed in restaurants. We were even banned from the synagogue! We would pass it on the way to work but could not go inside it. Jews were told to be off the streets before six o'clock. Our world, and our place in the world, got smaller and smaller.

The reality of the situation was that anger was building. It wasn't like a regular anger that spreads through an entire system of people; this anger was all on one side of the equation. Men like my father had no anger in them with which to push back, and that made the anger on the other side bolder, more provocative. It was incomprehensible to us, but to them, it seemed to make all of the sense in the world.

Home was not safe for long, either. We lived in a large house. It was central and well maintained. Personal items were now the property of the state. They came inside whenever they felt like it and took food and valuables. Then they would turn at the door and say they didn't trust us. They knew we were hiding something. We were still creating problems. That made them angry.

Our family business was stripped and taken away piece by piece. First, the police took away the contracts that we had with suppliers. They were not ours, they said. We were told when the store was to open and close.

This brings me to one of those strange moments in the middle of chaos. It was especially absurd. The Hungarian police made my father open the store on the Sabbath. They said there was no reason for keeping the store closed, and since our customs and practices meant nothing anymore, this would be an example to the community that their course of action would prevail. Our store would be open even if it were at gunpoint. My father followed command, but nobody came. Our store was usually a very busy place, but on the Sabbath, it was completely empty. Non-Jews wouldn't come into a Jewish neighborhood and enter a Jewish store. And the Jews stayed home. I think, even though my father was a very religious man, the fact that nobody showed up on those days made him smile.

The SS eventually published a list of Sighet's wealthiest families. They took Jewish leaders into custody and threatened to shoot them if the wealthy did not pay. Anger and threats from the Hungarian police, the German army, even the German SS became a pattern of living. But a line was soon crossed. Up until then, it was fine to just take things away. Words accompanied by corrupt laws were used to steal, take away dignity, and marginalize the Jewish people. In 1943, when I was a girl of fifteen, angry words were replaced by actions of violence. There were no repercussions; violence became the new form of communication. There was no debate. Instead, there was an argument that nobody would win. On the streets, Hungarian police beat my father as he walked to my family's store, and took his keys. People he was friendly with and those we had done business with for years just stood by and watched. The keys were not his, they told him. My father no longer allowed us to go to the store with him. Others were taken away by the secret police. Many were accused of hiding food and valuables. Many actually did for very good reasons. Our silence was the only thing that worked to dissuade them. There were stories of torture. There were stories of worse. I'm not sure if we did not believe them at the time because we were naïve or if we chose to actively deny the truth. After all, the truth had abandoned us in so many other areas.

At the end of 1942, the Hungarian government had made a law to deport to Poland all Jews who could not prove Hungarian citizenship. Any foreigners who were not from

Sighet were taken from their homes to the train station, where they were loaded into boxcars for the trip. Some families had been living in Sighet for generations. It was very heartbreaking for us to watch people forced into leaving their homes. People we had known for years were crying as they were escorted to the trains. It was a sad and terribly difficult time. We were powerless to help or to intercede at any level; there was nothing you could do. People were confused. Even after the deportation and with all the acts of anti-Semitism that were accruing in Sighet, we were still refusing to believe that it could become any worse than this.

They took away a popular rabbi, who everyone knew had spent his entire life in the town, because he could not prove his citizenship. Many people justified the act by saying, "Well, they just wanted to get rid of a popular community figure." I guess we needed to believe in the lesser of the injustices than the truth. We needed to believe in humanity because that's what we were taught.

I'll give an example of how the truth was a casualty of war in Sighet. Elie Wiesel writes about it in his book *Night*. Elie Wiesel and I were friends and neighbors when we were young, and his sister Beatrice and I became lifelong friends. This is an event that had extreme significance for him, and all of us who were there, and is worthy of taking a moment to repeat.

Another widely known resident, the caretaker of a synagogue, Moshe, who is the heart of this story, was taken away along with other Jews. I remember, two months after the people were taken, Moshe returned and created a ripple in our lives. He meant to sound an alarm, one that might wake us up and put us on a different road, but we did not listen. We did not recognize the truth when it hammered at our door.

Moshe spoke to the Jewish Council. He talked to his neighbors. He ran from one Jewish household to the next shouting, "Jews, listen to me! It's all I ask of you. No money, no pity, just listen to me!"

His story was impossible. It couldn't be true. The townspeople thought he was crazed or looking for sympathy, and we thought, *What an imagination he has!* Or sometimes, they pitied him and said, "Poor fellow, he's gone mad."

And as for Moshe, he wept. He knew the truth, and this was his warning to them: When the group of refugees crossed the border into Poland, the Gestapo, the German secret police, took charge of all of the Jews in the group of refugees. They were transferred onto trucks and driven to the forest in Galicia, near Kolomyya. There they were forced to dig pits. The pits were supposed to be deep enough to be latrines, but that was not the point. I'm sure you understand.

The job was finished. The Germans had each person approach the hole. The prisoner presented his neck to the soldier and was shot. Babies were thrown into the air and used as targets for machine gunners.

Moshe told them about a young man, Tobias, who begged to be shot before his sons. Another story was about a young girl named Malka, who took three days to die. Moshe told them how the German gunners had gotten impatient and started firing into the crowd. He had been hit in the leg, and they'd left him for dead.

This story sticks in my head not because of what it meant at the time. It was what it could have meant or maybe what it was supposed to have meant. It was one of those moments that passed so quickly. The simple and sad truth is that we didn't heed the message that was delivered to us.

Despite Moshe's plea, and all of the intimidating and corrupt conditions in Sighet, life went on for my family and friends. We still socialized. We were a family of twelve, so there was always a birthday to celebrate. Children played, couples got married, and we celebrated the Jewish holidays. I think we were all desperate for life to return to normal. Socializing gave us a temporary sense of security and hope. We made the best out of it.

SERPENT STREET / THE SIGHET GHETTO

Two sections of Sighet were divided, and our section was the larger one of them, on Serpent Street. One day in the spring, the Hungarian army began putting up barricades and barbed wire fences around these sections. Restrictions were already placed on our movement, and we were not allowed to go out except during certain times of the day. By this time, our family business had been taken away completely, so we no longer were able sell any goods. We had become captives in our own homes. Jews who lived in the countryside and other districts of Sighet were rounded up and forced to move into our sections. Three other families moved in with us to live in our home. Once the barbed wire fences and barricades were constructed, we were guarded day and night by the local Hungarian gendarmes and about fifty members of the Hungarian military. Both of the sections combined were only a few blocks long. The population in both areas grew to about thirteen thousand people. In some homes, there could be up to thirty people sharing living space. We were all in it together, so there was a calling by our Jewish leaders for great effort to create an organized humanitarian environment.

We were caught off guard, on purpose, of course, and we didn't know until much later that trickery and secrecy were enormously important to the Nazis' success and campaign to destroy us. We were still under the illusion that all would be okay and this would pass. Our recent past was clashing with shock and disbelief. It seemed to be hindering us from seeing what was right in front of us.

From the time I was born until the Nazis took over, my family, all of us, were in love with life. It wasn't that we didn't have our difficulties—we did—but our sense of community, decency, and humanity was very strong and very powerful. We knew right from wrong and how to treat people with dignity and respect. We didn't realize that life had seriously changed and that all the good—our family values, all our beliefs, and everything we had been taught—would be seriously challenged. God and these principles were all we had left to trust and get us through. Material possessions and small keepsakes that we had shared throughout my life were gone. All of them were gone.

Although I'm sure there were some, I really can't recall any acts of selfishness. Most of the people who moved into our sections were poor, and food had to be rationed. With so many people living under one roof, scheduling a day was a big responsibility that required cooperation from everyone. Your home, over time, becomes a sanctuary, a safe place for family privacy, a place to learn and grow with minimal interference. Our home was where we could just be ourselves and relax. In general, people often don't realize what they really have until it's taken from them. Having three families move into our home was just as traumatic for us as it was for them, and through much cooperation, we all had to adjust. My mother, my older sister Ety, and I helped organize different tasks and schedule the meals for everyone in the house. We had a shed outside, behind our house, where we kept lots of extra canned goods and food supplies that were meant for our business. I don't know if the Nazis knew we had the supplies, but they never bothered to look, so we were able to help people and make sure they didn't go hungry.

With all the overcrowding in our home, each family had to share the living facilities. At first it was chaotic, but after several days, we worked out a nice little routine that worked to benefit us all. Meals were our biggest concern, so my mother staggered each mealtime, starting early in the morning, so that each family was able to make its own meals and eat privately at separate times. Our home was now their home, and that's the way it went all throughout the Sighet ghetto.

We did our best to organize ourselves under the conditions we were given. Our leaders organized a Jewish Council, which was led by Rabbi Samu Danzig. They created a whole humanitarian system, upon which we all agreed, and it operated like a tiny city. I really think it was a testament to my family and to the Jews of Sighet. It was a testament to our determination. We refused to betray our principal beliefs and high standards in how we conducted ourselves toward one another and the rest of humanity. We were good, decent people, not the manipulated propaganda and untruths that Hitler and his followers had spread so disgustingly across Europe.

DEPORTATION / THE NAZI DECEIT

In March 1944, Adolf Eichmann arrived in Hungary to oversee the deportation of the Jews to Auschwitz. He was assigned by General Reinhard Heydrich, chairman of the Wannsee Conference, to set in motion and implement the Final Solution, the extermination of the Eastern European Jew. He was the commander of the Nazis' Sondereinsatzkommando (the special response unit of the German state police forces). It was a long and grand title for an organization of men who were essentially killers.

In May 1944, in a weeklong deportation process, 15,500 Jews were deported from Sighet to the Auschwitz concentration camp by the German SS and the Hungarian authorities.

It was very hot that day when the Hungarian government sent a representative to tell us the ghettos would be closed immediately. They said that a speedy deportation was being put into effect and that we should pack a few clothes and some food because we wouldn't be coming back. We were told we would be going to a work camp, but we weren't told our destination. We weren't allowed to ask questions. Asking where we were going or how long it would take to get there could get us beaten or even killed. And somehow, we were still under the illusion that all would be okay and this would pass.

I am still asked today how we were unaware that people were being murdered or how could we have been so naïve. Sometimes, that question almost feels more accusatory rather than a real need-to-know of the facts. The truth isn't that simple. I wish it was, but what is not understood is that if we thought for a second that within three days' travel time, our families and friends would be going to their deaths, or that most of the people I grew up with would be dead, of course we would have reacted in some way. However, that's how secret the murdering was. And sometimes, I ask myself if it was us, if we were we the ones who needed to wake up. The inhumanity and crimes that were being committed, along with the massive complicity that was running out of control across Europe, could have all been stopped instantly with one act of courage from any one of the ruling political powers. But waking up wasn't something *we* needed to do. The decision to support Hitler in whatever capacity would be something that millions would later realize and for most, I must say, disgracefully regret.

The next day, we were told we had to walk to the location of where the transport was. I'm not sure, but I believe it was about four miles. There were thousands of people walking as we left Serpent Street, and I wondered what they all must have been thinking. There were friends I had played with as a child, groups of people who fought to stay together, and families who hid away in the buildings as they waited for their turn to be sent to the transports. As I walked through this marvelous town in which I had grown up, I realized for the first time that it was all built with a divine purpose. For me, Sighet had an irresistible charm and a family intimacy. I had inhaled it all—the different shops and stores that were all snuggled together and which I had visited all my life and loved so much—and all of it lived deeply in my heart. As we all walked through town, people I recognized held hands and embraced each other, and there didn't appear to be any particular etiquette to it; it was spontaneous. Family social barriers broke down. People that were normally distant held hands; men clutched their children, sisters paired with brothers, and the old supported the young. I held hands with my mother for the first time since I was a little girl. My father and my younger brother, Mortho, held hands. And then, it would seem for no reason, we were holding someone else's hand, which is why touching seemed more important than ever. It was like everyone was saying what they always wanted to say to each other but never did, and it was all through touch and very few words.

As I walked, the memories flashed and left as quickly as they came. I felt they were being stolen by some strange unseen force. I couldn't seem to focus on anyone, though, and the longer we walked, the beauty of Sighet seemed to dull. Life in Sighet was all I knew. Step-by-step, it became a march instead of a walk. We were forced promptly along by the eager and always threatening Hungarian army and police. When we reached the border of the ghetto, it became almost like some kind of horrible parade. The people from town, the non-Jews, people we had known since childhood, watched as we deserted our homes, dragged our packs—our lives—out of town. People we had shared our lives with were now shouting out hateful anti-Semitic comments. They watched us through their windows, studying our misery. Some poked fun at us and scornfully smiled. Some looked away. Bless those who did.

The Hungarian gendarmes and police carried rifles and batons. I know there is no way to explain what drives a man to push around women and children, treat them like cattle, but there were definitely two types of policemen in Hungary. The first was the kind that would look at us and instantly despise us. A person who can look directly into the eyes of misery and see a target for more punishment is a terrible person to meet. I tried not to see these people, even though they saw me (today, I find peace by letting go of their faces in my memories). The other type of policeman would look away if I looked at him. These were the ones I pitied. It seems strange that I would be in the position to pity even when everything was being taken away from me, but I pitied them regardless.

In these brief moments, my observation of these policemen who wouldn't look at me appeared as a sign and a microcosm of Hitler's evil agenda, which I had never experienced before. This was a new experience for me to see the betrayal of one's own self, and I was beginning to recognize a suffering in some underneath it. Peer pressure, fear, murder, and intimidation by a few were causing millions of people to act in ways that they might not normally behave.

The Hungarian girl, my first real friend, and whom I spoke about briefly at the beginning of my story, would become a memory that at times still haunts me today. She lived just down the street from my family and me, and we went to primary school together. She was someone I had played with every day, and we shared our childhood dreams together. We had drifted apart as we got older, but I would run into her from time to time, and we would catch up and share a smile and a laugh.

The day our deportation orders were enforced and we were marched through the streets, I spotted her standing together with a hateful crowd. As I got closer, and just before she saw me, I could see she was participating in the shouting. When she saw me, I knew she knew who I was. How could she forget what we shared? I knew what joy looked like on her face. I searched for some sign of support from her, but all I could see was her newfound hatred. She completely rejected me. I was sure she would have even denied knowing me, but then she coldly smiled, waved, and laughed wickedly at me. I didn't recognize her anymore. My friend was gone, lost in the madness. A sadness and pain crept over my whole body. I felt weak and small, almost like I was rejecting my own self.

When we finally arrived at the train station, there was no passenger train. It wasn't a train at all; instead, it was like wagons or boxcars, something you would load cattle into. I was with my mother and father, my brothers Mendal and Mortho, and my three sisters Hedy, Rose, and Ancy. Ety, my oldest sister, had stayed behind with her husband and was to be placed on a later transport. My brother Lazar had made a decision early on to leave Sighet for Russia to try to break away from all the anti-Semitism. And because men were required, at age eighteen, to serve in the Hungarian military, my brothers Haskell and Joseph had been assigned to the Hungarian Second Army, which was made up of mostly Jews. They were not with us on the train. After anti-Jewish laws were set into place in 1938, Jews who were in the Hungarian military were regarded as unreliable and could not be trusted to carry a weapon. As a replacement for their guns, Jews were given shovels and pickaxes. They were supervised by the anti-Semitic Hungarian military, but it really was just Nazi slave labor. They exploited Jews by forcing them to work in copper mines or clear minefields with other so-called undesirables.

It was very traumatic at the train station. I'll never forget when Rose was separated and told to go to another wagon. There were seventy people in each wagon, without exception, and Rose would have made the count seventy-one. I just looked at her in shock.

She said, "Don't worry, Klara. I'll be okay."

I knew her love for me and that she was more concerned about me than herself. She had taken care of me most of my life. I couldn't protest; the Hungarian gendarmes didn't care. If we were caught speaking, they would beat us. People were pushed and shoved by the gendarmes as they crammed us all into the wagon. Then, the door slammed shut and was locked from the outside. There wasn't a handle or any way to open the doors from the inside. There was only darkness and a horrible silence as my eyes struggled to see. A sliver of light came through the wooden slats of the wagon's walls. Almost immediately, the wagon became warm with body heat. There was no water on board, and the Hungarians in charge wouldn't give us anything to drink. Instead of a toilet, there were only disgusting metal pails to use. They hated us and made sure we knew it. We huddled together, and I could see my parents were exhausted. For the first time in my life, I was deeply concerned for them. People spoke only when necessary and mostly among themselves. Fear filtered through, mixed with feelings of tremendous respect and courage. It seemed like forever before the train started to move, and I felt a small bit of relief when it finally did. I desperately wanted to go back home. I could see a small bit of light shining on my father's face, which showed tiny bits of sweat, sprinkled with dust. As I gazed up at him, I saw the holy man that he was, and I unconsciously let my mind wander. A memory of my father that I deeply needed overtook me.

As a child, I kept my ears open; I wanted to know everything. In Europe, if a girl wanted to get married, she'd have to have a dowry, and a boy definitely wouldn't marry her unless she had one. My father knew of a beautiful couple who were dating, and they couldn't get married because the girl's family was very poor. My father consulted a rabbi, who sometimes acted more like a judge. If you had some difficulties or a dispute with someone and it wasn't necessary to go to court, the rabbi would listen and decide who was right and who was wrong. My father really wanted to help the couple but couldn't afford to pay for the girl's dowry all at once. Instead, he solicited the counsel of this judge, and they came to an agreement. My father would give a monthly stipend to count toward the girl's dowry. Of course, he had to hide all this from my mother, as she would never have agreed. I never knew what the exact amount was. After the Hungarian gendarmes took over Sighet, my father was not able to go to our store anymore. If he tried, he would have been harassed and beaten for having a beard. The Hungarians hated what the beard represented and threatened to cut his off. My father taught me the beard is hair that grows down from the head and is the bridge between the mind and heart. The beard—or the bridge—carries thoughts, actions, philosophies and practice, worthy intentions, and worthy deeds to the heart.

No longer able to make the trip to the store, my father missed a payment to the girl's family. Soon, we received a note, delivered by a courier, from the rabbi, which stated that my father had missed a payment.

My mother, still unknowing of the agreement, was shocked. She said, "What kind of payment?" That's when she found out that my father, may he rest in peace, had promised to give so much money per month to this girl so she could get married. My mother asked him very calmly, "Ignatiu, how on earth can you do a thing like that? We have five girls who will need a dowry, and to give money to a complete strange girl, how can you do that?"

My father answered quite rationally, saying how much in love the couple was and how badly they wanted to be married. "I felt so sorry for them. I had to do it."

In order to keep our good reputation, my mother continued to pay the money every month, until the Nazis took away the remainder of what we had.

I'm not sure how long I was lost in this wonderful memory nor what brought me back to the present. But when I came back, a terrifying feeling came over me, a feeling I had never felt before. That's when I realized that I would have to pay a high price for that memory, and the price was pain and suffering. Now our world, the one that I loved so much, was gone forever; there would be no going back. A new life had been created for us, one that was constructed by a demagogue and madman.

While on the train, nobody knew of our destination; all we were told was that we had been selected for resettlement and work. The Hungarians took us as far as a town called Kassa, which is about 130 miles from Sighet, on the border of Czechoslovakia. Our pleas for just a simple drink of water were completely ignored, and it was terribly hot. Many of the older people in our wagon passed out from lack of water and heat exhaustion.

When we arrived, the Germans took over control of the train but not before the Hungarians stole the rest of any valuables we had. They laughed and said, "You're going to be shot anyway."

After the Germans took control of the transport, they opened the doors and handed us water in metal buckets. Was it a small act of humanity? Or was it all a deception to keep us calm? We were not allowed to leave the wagons for any reason. It was such a horrible, horrible experience. I'm not sure how long we were there before the door slammed shut once more. We were moving again, and somehow I managed to drift in and out of sleep.

During the trip, my memories of the past became cloudy, and it was as if I was unable to recall anything enjoyable. For some reason, I began thinking about Dr. Younger, who was a well-known Jewish doctor in Sighet. Dr. Younger's practice was taken away, and he was stripped of his license to practice medicine. On the day he and his family were to be moved from their home and into the ghetto, he gave his children poison. Then he gave it to his wife. After that, he took it himself. All four bodies were found by the very people who persecuted them, the Hungarian gendarmes.

The ghetto was no stranger to death for my family either. The business owned by the brother of Ety's husband was confiscated. He was a very important, rich, and generous man before the war. But when he lost his company, it completely wiped him out financially. When he and his family moved into the ghetto, he only lasted two days. He couldn't adapt. He blamed himself for the loss and then killed himself with a gun that he had smuggled in with his family's belongings. As he was so well respected, everyone mourned for him.

These tragic incidents were things that I hadn't spent too much time thinking about when they happened, but now they appeared beyond my control and haunted me, forcing me to look and listen to my surroundings. Riding on that train, in the scorching May heat with not a drop of water or a place to cover your own waste, was like pity itself was dead. Sympathy had died in those first steps outside of our home, and memories that I thought were long gone had come back to challenge me.

We had never been considered part of the Hungarian or Romanian people, and now that we were no longer identified as Hungarian or Romanian, the last ties to commonality had been cut. Now that we had been sent away, there was no reason for anyone to feel anything for us. We barely had the strength to feel anything for ourselves. Everyone had run out of food by the third day of the transport. We sat on our belongings, or stood packed together in the dark. Nobody spoke; it was silent. All the crying and moaning of the past days had, somewhere in the dark, slipped through the cracks in the wood and onto the tracks, and had been left far behind.

There was no room in the car for anything extra except the idea of death, which traveled with us. I could see that for some, it was becoming a more welcome thought with each passing day. The wagon was a coffin that just hadn't yet been put into the ground.

We arrived at our new destination on the third night. The other passengers and I got off the train and slowly slipped through the gates of the death camp in darkness. The only sound was the train as it let loose its huge amount of steam. At this point, the one thing I knew for certain was that wherever we were was not going be in our best interest.

DR. JOSEF MENGELE / THE MURDERER IN WHITE

Much has been written about Dr. Josef Mengele. The one point that all seem to agree upon is that he was one of the most evil men to be documented in modern times. That Mengele became one of the greatest mass murderers of the twentieth century, causing the deaths of thousands of people through mass gassings, medical experiments, and direct killings, is a mystery that has been researched and written about for decades. The incredible mystery is and always has been that there is nothing in Mengele's early childhood that would indicate or suggest any justification as to what he would become. This would, to a great extent, aid in developing his legend. That being said, Mengele became who he became deliberately.

He strategically chose who and what he wanted to become and became it. From the time he was awarded his PhD from the University of Munich for his thesis titled "Racial Morphological Research on the Lower Jaw Section of Four Racial Groups," to his indoctrination in 1937, and appointment as research assistant at the Third Reich Institute for Heredity, Biology, and Racial Purity at the University of Frankfurt, he gravitated with zeal toward the darkest sides of the Nazi Party. In 1938, Mengele was admitted into the Nazi Party, where he developed the reputation as an enthusiastic official party member who was completely committed to Hitler's racist ideology. In October 1939, he joined the Wehrmacht, the armed forces of Nazi Germany. In 1940, Mengele joined the medical corps of the Waffen-SS, where he was appointed to the Race and Resettlement Office in occupied Poland. From there, in 1942, Mengele earned his second Iron Cross, the symbol of recognition of extreme bravery on the battlefield, by pulling two soldiers out of a burning tank while under enemy fire. That same year, he was reposted to the Race and Resettlement Office in Berlin, where, as he was a celebrated war hero, he was given the rank of captain.

Dr. Josef Mengele arrived at the Auschwitz concentration camp on May 30, 1943. He was thirty-two. With the benefit of an impeccable and commendable war record, Mengele's reputation was welcomed at Auschwitz with respect and authority.

Josef Mengele had passed all the rites of passage that were required of an indispensable Nazi and exceptional doctor. No other doctor at Auschwitz had received the battlefield awards that he had received for his service on the Russian front. At Auschwitz, Mengele proudly displayed his Iron Cross medals for all to see. With a captain's rank and his elite badge of honor, Mengele had an unquestionable superior advantage. Mengele firmly believed in Hitler's master plan to rid the European Jew from Europe, and he pursued and accelerated the process with extreme fanaticism. Almost always at the selection ramp when new transports would arrive, Mengele became known as a selection specialist. Along with his own plan to become a genetic purifier, Mengele would perfect the selection process at Auschwitz as he became the chief orchestrator over life and death. At the ramp, it was he who would decide who would live and who would die. Described by camp survivors as a tall, handsome Hollywood actor–type who was always impeccably dressed, Mengele was blessed with a magnetic personality and carried with him an air of confidence. One camp survivor described Mengele as a man who cast his spell on the new arrivals at the ramp, smiling and joking with you and creating a safe and comfortable environment where as little as five minutes later would have you walking to the gas chambers.

Prisoners who survived the ramp would, in a very short time, find that Dr. Josef Mengele was not a practitioner of medicine at all. His medical solutions for complaints or ailments would almost always be torture, shootings, and mass gassings, sending tens of thousands of healthy, defenseless people to their deaths. During Mengele's twenty-one months as a chief medical officer at Auschwitz, he would build the reputation as one of the most terrifying men in modern history.

Mengele put into use what his mentor, Professor Otmar Freiherr von Verschuer, taught him at the Third Reich Institute for Heredity, Biology, and Racial Purity at the University of Frankfurt. Professor Verschuer trained and encouraged Mengele to support and practice what he termed "race hygiene." In actuality, it is a criminal idea, a fancy intellectual medical term used to justify intolerance, indifference, and mass murder.

After stripping away all of the reputation, fascination, and the dark glorification, Dr. Josef Mengele was nothing more than an egomaniac, a coward, and an intellectual bully. He was a talented man of privilege who, at an early age, knew what he wanted and directed his own life accordingly at every opportunity. Always in a matter-of-fact way, Mengele chose evil over good, darkness over light, and death over life, which caused tens of thousands of innocent men, women, and children to suffer and die by his hand. At Auschwitz, Mengele would become only one thing, "the Murderer in White."

AUSCHWITZ-BIRKENAU
THE FINAL SOLUTION / A
SYLLABUS OF DEATH

Of course, we hadn't known it at the time, but when we arrived at our destination, we realized the SS had already been preparing for our murder. I learned later on, that about an hour before our arrival, the big generators that powered the crematoriums had started up, and smoke swirled from the giant chimneys. Armed with a textbook syllabus of death, the SS knew our arrival times, and the inescapable Auschwitz killing machine was set into motion.

Everything that we were about to experience was a deliberate deception, a predetermined show with all the actors in place to play their parts. One by one, I could hear the boxcar doors of the train being unlocked and opened. The noise got closer and closer; then suddenly, our door slid open into blackness. The sound was what hit me first. The three days we spent traveling in silence felt like we had been in a pressure chamber, and the shrill and sudden noises of whistles, screams, children crying, whips, and the occasional crack of a gun were our introduction to Auschwitz.

Accompanied by armed guards, the SS ordered a number of veteran prisoners to meet people at the train to help with taking our belongings. Unsympathetically, we were pushed and guided toward the selection ramps like cattle. We had no idea what a selection was or what it meant, but these prisoners and guards did. Prisoners who failed to participate would be killed without delay.

Humanity spilled out onto the railroad fields. It was like an explosion of sound and light. Spotlights defined the outer walls of our new prison. Razor wire glinted on the edges of this new cage. To understand this place at first sight, you would have to be a monster. What was confusion on our side was commonplace on the other. Guards and old-timers (prisoners who had been there for years) met the cars with their duties. I looked closely at the faces of the Auschwitz trustees for some kind of reassurance that we would be okay, that things would get better, but I got nothing; instead, vacant faces rushed us along.

A German soldier patrolled the train and barked, "Leave your suitcases and packages behind."

Our luggage was taken by the prisoners, but by this time, it just seemed to me like a burden anyway. I had no more attachment to my bags at all; I couldn't even remember what I had put in them. I do know that all of the luggage was sent to the main Auschwitz camp, where everything was sorted, and anything of value was taken by the Nazis. Auschwitz was massive in size, and at the time, there was no way of me knowing how big it actually was. Its size was of a small city, but in reality, no one was able to move around freely because it was a death camp controlled by the German SS.

We were moved along quickly. Everyone was ordered to line up in front of the train cars. The men were quickly separated from the women and children. I could see a few Red Cross vans waiting to take away the sick.

An SS guard spoke out to us. He said, "Stay calm. There is no need to be alarmed. You are going to be showered and disinfected, and then you will rejoin your families."

Then we were put into lines. There were five women and five men in each. I don't know how, but my sister, Rose, found us and lined up with us. She was terrified. I could tell she had been crying. Next they separated the men from us, and they were ordered to move and reform their lines just on the other side of the yard. That was the last time I saw my brother Mendal, who was moved with the other men.

I couldn't help but notice people being helped inside the Red Cross vans. That seemed to give me a small bit of comfort. Of course, I learned later anyone who was taken by the Red Cross vans was taken straight to the gas chambers. I saw just a glimpse of my youngest brother, Mortho's, coat disappearing along the same path forward to the gates in the dark. His face was in shadow. I knew my father must have been on the other side of him, because he was looking away from me. Mortho looked like a fully grown man. Even though he was only fourteen, he was taller than most of the guards. He had developed his mind and spirit into those of an adult. Mortho, to me, was the face of the tragedy of Auschwitz, even long after the fires had stopped burning. The sense, the beauty, and the loss were there in his eyes at that moment. I would have seen them if only he'd turned his face. I should have called out. What would I have said to him? I might have teased him for being so tall, or I might have told him to be careful. Hopefully, I would have been able to say something meaningful or worthy of our final words on Earth. We all must make an effort when we know it is the last time we'll ever see a loved one. I know, because when he slipped away into the crowd, I felt like I had let him down. As we made our way to the gates, I fell on the gravel. I wanted to stop for a minute, but the pain immediately brought me back to my task, which was to move forward. My mother helped me to stand up. I said nothing to her. This turned out to be another silent good-bye.

As we pressed into the camp, old-timers pushed against the current toward the trains. They wore black striped uniforms. Some, mainly the Polish, were political prisoners and wore red-triangle armbands. These were the Jews who had been in the camp for years. They knew not to speak Yiddish because it was too close to German, and the messages they'd try to deliver could not be overheard without punishment. Instead, they spoke Polish and told our group to translate it back to the others in Hungarian or Romanian. Their message was unthinkable.

"Leave your children," they said. "They will kill you if you stay with your children. The children are lost either way."

You can imagine the haggard forms of the concentration camp coming out of the shadows and screams of the night that followed this message. Nobody believed them. Still, mothers clutched their babies closer, and they pulled their children in tighter around them. There were a few grandmothers in the group who spoke Polish and heard the warnings. They took the children from their daughters and saved their daughters' lives. This might have seemed like a form of defiance; however, I met some of these mothers in the camp. I didn't meet a single one who felt like their lives had truly been saved.

One woman along the side of the tracks refused to join the lines. She screamed like an animal. A group of soldiers crowded around her, and she fell silent. They carried her away. I stopped looking around me. I looked forward. My ears rang from her screaming.

There was a point where flashlights were grouped around an intimidating figure. This is when I first met Josef Mengele. There in the dark, it felt like I was back in the movie theater in Sighet. He was the most handsome man I'd ever seen in person. To this day, I remember him as a matinee idol who had stepped off of the screen and into a real-life horror story. This was the most feared man in Auschwitz. You had to have a special relationship with evil to be called that here. Camp survivors gave Mengele a suitable title: the Angel of Death.

I was told that he met every train arrival, but all I know is that he met ours and made his selection. He stood tall, was very neat and superior, and had complete self-confidence. Nobody doubted that he was in charge. His uniform was impeccable, right down to the white cotton gloves and shiny black boots. The gloves were impossibly white for the times. Nothing around him was so clean. He also carried a riding stick in his right hand, which he used to direct us where to go. He would point and send someone either left or right. Why left? Why right? No one knew how or why he chose as he did. To us, it seemed as though he was merely separating people. He pushed all of the old and young into the track to our right. Sometimes he asked questions before making his judgments. I've tried to imagine that he liked to think that there was some kind of science to his mission, a logic that made his deadly convictions part of the natural order and therefore true. He was a man of science. He was a doctor. Although, we didn't know he was a doctor at the time, and he didn't feel obligated to introduce himself. He could quickly diagnose anyone set before him, even five at a time.

He pointed his riding stick at my sister Rose. "You are sisters?" Although he asked, it was more of a statement than a question.

"Yes, sir," Rose answered.

"Someone should take care of your mother. You to the left, go with her." He pointed at Ancy. She was the beauty of our family. She was twenty-six years old and had long blond hair. Her smile was known all over Sighet. There was something about it that caught the attention of everyone, not just the boys. Maybe it was that potential that caught the attention of Mengele. Ancy was relieved to go with our mother. She always wanted to go where she might be of the most help. I can't remember her last smile because I still kept my eyes focused straight ahead of me. And with that, Mengele separated us. I went with two of my sisters, Hedy and Rose, and went to the left, while Ancy and my mother went to the right. I never saw them again except in my dreams.

But there was no comfort in that for a long time. Where we were headed, even dreams were not much of a place for solace. That night, within hours of our arrival, my father and mother, my younger brother, Mortho, and my sister Ancy had been selected by Mengele to die in the gas chamber simply because they were Jews and served no purpose to the SS agenda. There was nothing that could be done. Their death sentence may well have been decided three days prior, the day we boarded the train. At the time, we had no idea. Mengele smiled and reassured us that we would be taken by bus and that we would see them tomorrow. That's what he said. Why, at this point, I listened and believed, I don't know.

We lined up to the right to complete the selection. The three of us, Rose, Hedy, and I, made it past that line, but really, there were only two people and a shadow. That shadow was me. That was the selection process at Auschwitz. Little did I know Josef Mengele and I would meet again.

THE DEMORALIZATION PROCESS

From this point on, Rose, Hedy, and I were fortunately together as we continued on through the dehumanizing process of Auschwitz. For us, it seemed chaotic to walk through those gates as dogs barked and German soldiers with machine guns yelled orders. But it was all very well organized and anything but chaotic. We were marched quickly to a wooden building—a bathhouse—by armed soldiers with dogs. There were open latrines below it, and it smelled of urine and vomit.

I held the hand of my sister Hedy. She told me something that was repeated to me so many times during my containment at Auschwitz: "Do what they say, and you will be fine."

Being in that place was very strange. It was exactly the opposite of how I felt. I began to doubt the meaning of everything. My own words did not seem to mean anything. The words of my fellow prisoners made no sense either.

I asked them, "When are we going to see our parents?"

And they answered in very hard and heartless ways. They said, "Do you see that flame there?"

I looked up as they pointed to a very tall smokestack made of red brick. I saw flames and smoke that rolled upward, out the top, and into the night sky.

"That's where your parents are. Your parents are dead."

These were Jewish girls. We thought they were just crazy. We didn't know what they were talking about. We had no idea that, unfortunately, they were telling the truth.

They always told us, "Do what they say, and you will be fine." But that couldn't be true. I looked around the bathhouse for some sign that something, *anything*, was fine. I saw a sign that said that people were to keep themselves clean at all times. I imagined it came from another time, when people had a choice. I bet the sign maker actually thought he was putting a helpful suggestion onto the wall with his work. He had no idea that his words would be hung in a place where words had only one meaning: do what it says, or be killed.

People who control words control everything. Words in the society of Auschwitz had weight. The real things that crushed our spirits were the words.

I didn't have control over what happened next. We were told to strip off our clothes while four or five male soldiers watched. Then, we were put under streams of water that went from scalding hot to stinging cold, depending upon which nozzle we stood under. I had no control over how I looked either. We were quickly ushered to the next line, where we stood naked and waited to have our hair sheared off while big German soldiers stood guard.

My sisters and I had beautiful long hair, and for a woman or young girl, cutting off our hair was like stealing our dignity or beauty. Our image was stripped away. In my home, for us, hair was a ritual. We spent hours washing each other's hair, braiding each other's hair. We brushed each other's hair, combed each other's hair; we put it up and giggled and laughed while we decorated it. We would experiment with it, play with it, and cut it. We did everything to it. Our hair was the mark of our femininity, which bonded us as sisters so that we could blossom into women. And now, all our hair was cut off, from head to toe, by a gruff Polish prisoner who looked and acted like a machine. I felt my history disappear with the gift that God gave me, along with my experience as a human being. I didn't recognize Hedy and Rose anymore.

The Polish prisoner who cut my hair noticed tears in my eyes and coldly stated, "If you cry here, you die here."

We were given gray dresses made from the thinnest fabric I'd ever seen, a pair of wooden clog shoes, and a wooden bowl with a hole in it so we could tie it to ourselves. Our bowls were our lives. We were told if we lost them, we wouldn't eat. I also had no control over how I spoke. By that, I mean I had to control how I spoke. We couldn't speak above a whisper for fear of being beaten, although the orders that were shouted at us were meant to control our every move. I looked around everywhere for some sign of sense in this place. There was steam on the inside of the windows so that I couldn't see out of them. There was no escape from this place. Everybody was trapped, and everything was taken away from us. The salvation of this observation would have to wait.

And then the tattoo. Numbers were painfully inked onto our arms. Mine was A-7845. This was the Nazis' way of permanently dehumanizing us, especially for traditional Jewish families like ours, where tattooing is prohibited. Our father had taught us that our bodies are worthy of respectful treatment by others and ourselves. He taught us that we must not mistreat our bodies and that our bodies were made in *tzelem Elokim* (in God's image). In the Jewish tradition, the body should not be marked arbitrarily or foolishly. From that moment on, Klara, the happy young girl from Sighet, was gone. My sisters were also tattooed, and I could see the pain in their eyes. I felt horrible for them. We found out later that before the Jews had been branded with a number, some of them would sneak between the different sections of the camp. Some people were able to reunite with their families or seek out the comfort of a friend through this freedom. The number put an end to that. We heard a story that if one number—one girl—was missing from a barrack, the entire block was sent to the crematorium. The Nazis had perfected the process of nonsense in language, and so they sought to conquer numbers as well. They reminded us of this with the signs on the walls and the numbers on our arms.

As we were marched away from the bathhouse and into the camp, I knew I had left my old reality forever. Any innocence that I might have had left had been shattered with the tattoo, A-7845. The only real things we would experience, and could possibly experience, from this point on were death, suffering, hunger, and pain. There was a difference between a concentration camp and an extermination camp. The realization slowly crept upon us that we were now in the belly of Auschwitz. From top to bottom, Auschwitz was the Nazis' supreme extermination camp.

LIFE AND DEATH AT AUSCHWITZ

The extermination camp at Auschwitz was built on four hundred acres in the countryside, beside the Soła River, near Krakow, Poland. When we arrived, it was springtime. Sometimes, the weather would be very hot, but it was more commonly wet, dreary, and foggy. At night and during the winter season, the weather was bitterly cold, with quite an accumulation of snow on the ground. When it rained, the ground turned into mud, which made it next to impossible to walk in the wooden clogs the SS gave us. Most of the time, the sky was ash gray. There was no plant life, no animal life, and no grass growing, not a living thing. Ironically, the town of Birkenau was named after a beautiful tree that had lived on the land that we were now on. The Germans destroyed the small town of Birkenau, completely killing all of the birch trees in order to build the extermination camp. They kept the name of the tree as the name of our camp—Birkenau—which for me symbolized life, and they mocked it by murdering. The buildings had no personality. Although the land we were on was once beautiful, it felt like they had built this compound on a wasteland. There were a number of camps, which were set up in sections, and each section had barracks or blocks. My sisters and I were assigned to the B Camp at Auschwitz-Birkenau. Each block had female prisoners put in charge by the SS to supervise us and to implement the Nazi agenda. Though it was brutally and rigidly organized, it was always terrifyingly unpredictable and could change at any moment, which was the way it was intended to be. We were marched to our section of the barracks, and they were very poorly kept. Auschwitz was completely inhospitable, and the ways in which we were treated there were awful. Ten girls had to sleep in one bed, and there were hardly any blankets. There were no pillows at all. It was a horrible, miserable way to treat a human being, what they did. The beds were so tight and small that if someone wanted to turn over while they were sleeping, all of the girls had to. It was so horrible!

On the way to the barracks, Rose asked the Polish girls who were in charge when we were going to see our parents.

They all said virtually the same thing. They told us, "You will meet them tomorrow; they are waiting for you."

I'm not sure if it was to save us from pain or just to make their job easier. They certainly didn't want to tell us the truth. Looking back, I believe that they probably saved a lot of people's lives by not telling us and others the truth. I'm sure all order over who was in charge would have disappeared. We had to wait to console ourselves and then answer questions about our own life-and-death situations. Whether it was for them or for us, decisions for prisoners at Auschwitz were based on survival; small mistakes could mean instant death. We were given a limited orientation to our surroundings. There wouldn't be anyone to show us the ins and outs that could help us endure. Why would they? Auschwitz was an extermination camp, an organized system of fear that used unpredictability as one of its tools to help support its policy of mass murder. We would have to adapt quickly if we wanted to survive.

The barracks were completely dark at night, and we could hardly see. We slept ten girls to a bunk. The bunks were just slats of wood across a rickety frame. Girls crashed through them regularly. It's strange, but the girl who fell almost always suffered less than the girl she fell upon. My sisters and I were on the top bunks, which were the least desirable because it could get extremely cold at night. Cold air would swirl in through the gaps in the sidewalls. By being on the top, our bodies acted like radiators. The air blew over us and down onto the others. Our body heat helped when it became unbearably cold. On my first night, I dreamed of my old life. I remember this clearly. On the first night, I actually believed that I would wake up in old Sighet before the war, when life was wonderful. After the first night, lying there in complete darkness, no matter how hard I tried to believe that the dream was real, I couldn't.

The dreams of home came less often after a week had passed. And finally, they stopped altogether.

"Aufstehen! Aufstehen!" they would yell in German, which means "Get up! Get up!" That was how our first morning began. I couldn't see these people with the loud, harsh voices, but I could feel them moving toward our bunk, and then they were yelling again, *"Aufsteten! Aufstehen!"*

Women scurried off their bunks, some falling from the top in an attempt to follow commands. This is when we met our block senior. She was also called *Blockalteste*, or "block leader." Our block senior had a sister named Lilly who acted as her secretary. They were both from Czechoslovakia. The Blockaltestes were prisoners picked by the SS as trusties to supervise us and were given various duties and responsibilities. In exchange, they got to live in much better conditions compared to us. They had their own sleeping quarters and plenty of food and other privileges. There were about six hundred women in our block. Each block was broken down into sections; there were six to twelve women who were assigned to help bring the food back to the block and to wake us up in the morning.

We stood in front of our bunks, and it was the first time we actually saw the room that was our sleeping prison. I thought, *This doesn't look like a prison at all.* Of course, I had never been to a jail or prison, so my idea of one was only through books and pictures that I had read about. I had slept very little that first night, and I could tell Hedy and Rose hadn't slept well either. We hardly recognized each other with our hair cut so short. Our three-day journey from the ghetto to here was such a surreal nightmare, and we were still exhausted. But what we were about to confront was the real nightmare. It would be with us awake or asleep. No matter what we did, we would be powerless to make it go away.

Auschwitz would become a world of constant hypervigilance that would take on a life of its own. It would become a massive world of people, all with individual stories, in a life-and-death race with time. Life expectancy at Auschwitz was usually three to four months. The camp was surrounded by a huge electrical fence, with razor wire at the top, and a moat surrounding the fence. Guard towers were placed in strategic spots, and armed SS guards with dogs patrolled the grounds with shoot-to-kill orders for anyone who tried to escape. At night, a few women prisoners were assigned to make sure no one left the barracks or that no one tried to steal anything.

My first thought was, *This looks like the kind of place a farmer would put animals to shelter them at night.* I happened to be right. Our new quarters were prefabricated horse stables that had been shipped in from the Russian front. The wood was dry and dead. It creaked at the slightest push of the hand or foot. The room was completely barren, no toilets or running water. There was no clutter in the corners. Dust was the only thing that collected in this place. The room reflected that perfectly. On cold nights, the air was so filled with frost that it looked like we were all smoking. Every day, at first light, we were awakened by screaming whistles. Time was not measured by clocks for us; time just seemed to fold into itself and disappear at Auschwitz. We were rushed out into the courtyard. My thin gray dress was barely enough to shield the wind from my body, and it definitely did not hold in any of the warmth. I remember staring, for a long time, at the smokestack that billowed in the center of the camp. *That place must be warmer*, I thought.

I turned to one of the Polish prisoners and asked when I was going to see my mother. She shrugged. Her face had no compassion. I was worried that my father might not be able to stand the cold of the night. I knew my mother would find a way to make this place make more sense. I had so many questions for them both. But they were questions that would go unanswered.

The Polish girl had a friend, and she saw that I was confused and worried. She pointed to the smokestack and said, "You see, your parents are there."

I couldn't believe how mean the girl was, and her utter lack of compassion. My sister Hedy quickly moved us away from her. We would have done anything to get away from that horrible woman. How could she say such a thing? I think I learned to stop asking questions that day. It was the strangest kind of cruelty, a cruelty I had never experienced before, and it came from our own.

While we were nevertheless alive, the SS took pleasure in keeping us as uncomfortable as possible. Even when the SS was not in our presence, which was rare, there was always an unspoken threat that they were close by and would treat us brutally. We knew at any moment that things could change drastically for any reason. It might have been a few weeks before we understood that our parents and our younger brother, Mortho and sister Ancy were, in fact, dead. That truth, that pain, was so unbearable that we had to find a way to cry without the SS seeing us. The familiar camp slogan, "You cry, you die," rang in our minds. The temptation to lash out was so strong that if I hadn't had Hedy and Rose, I'm not sure if I would have been able to keep from doing something foolish. My mind drifted to Mengele and the night we arrived. He was their killer, and from now on, I would keep an eye out for him. After that, my sisters and I made it a point to console and comfort people who came to Auschwitz after we did. Now we would know from experience whose relatives were murdered by the deceitful SS and Mengele.

The block leaders were also in charge of the work details and could be very cruel. I never understood their brutality. I do understand that it was part of the Auschwitz system. Some were criminals and were picked because they were characteristically brutal. There were also the Blockaltestes that tried to help you. Most Blockaltestes had lived through years of hell. I say this because I don't want anyone to think that I am blaming them. Blame is a concept of luxury. When you have nothing but your life, blame means nothing. My mother would never come back regardless of whom I blamed. The SS would not change their actions even with the whole world in judgment of them.

Perhaps I still don't know how to put my parents' death into words. In my mind, I still see them. I still see their smiles, and I hear their voices. Their memory leads me to a very personal love and to the truth, but I don't think I will ever be able to explain how that is so. I can only relate the conditions of their sudden deaths. I can show you how this was seen through the prism of a seventeen-year-old girl. Maybe through this retelling, you will learn some of the truth that took me so many years to learn. Auschwitz was the great stealer of humanity, but it could never steal my humanity, my core foundation, the humanity instilled in us by our remarkable parents.

We had to make our beds following very strict rules and in a military-type fashion called *Bettenbau*. We were required to make our beds perfectly, and if they weren't made perfectly, you could be severely beaten. It was always a very anxious time for us. Keeping yourself clean was hard because there were only a few places to wash and thousands of women. After the beds were made, people were sent to wash and use the toilets, which were nothing more than long benches with holes in them that ran down the middle of a hovel-like building. There was no privacy at all; the toilets were completely open, which created unsanitary conditions for us all. After that, breakfast was brought. Breakfast was a slice of bread to eat and a cup of black coffee to drink. Many of us didn't eat or drink on our first day. The condition of the food was comparable to food you had picked out of a trash can. The coffee tasted like it had been recycled through a human system a few times before it was served. The food actually makes me smile when I think of it now. It was so putrid that it still evokes emotion from me to this day. I turn it into a smile because emotions have to come out somehow. I began to lose weight from that first day. This may not sound important, but it is what eventually led to my selection to be taken to the showers, killed, and cremated. This action was still months away, though, and although I connect it through hunger and suffering, there was no easy way out of Auschwitz.

That first day in the yard was the hardest. We were ordered outside for morning roll call, where we lined up in rows of ten. Lineup was where the SS really showed off their power and cruelty. They always used the opportunity to reinforce to us their brutal control. We were kept in line, sometimes for hours, and just waited. Some people were too weak to stand, so they were yanked out of line and were taken straight to the gas chamber.

Hedy, Rose, and I stayed close together; I could see anxiety on their faces, and I'm sure they felt mine as well. I kept being distracted by my new tattoo. We all carefully examined each other's tattoos; it felt so strange that I constantly looked down at it and tried to wipe it off. We couldn't realize the depth of its meaning at the time. When my sisters and I spoke with each other, we spoke softly, in a protected whisper, because at this point, we didn't know who we could trust. I think our adrenaline was keeping us all going, because we hadn't eaten a meal or slept for days.

I looked out over a sea of women as we all nervously waited for the sun to come up again. The Blockaltestes quickly ordered us to get in lines of five. Anybody who hesitated or didn't move quickly enough was beaten. The sun didn't come up that day. The sky just turned to ash gray. First, the Blockaltestes counted the lines. Then the SS counted us. Nobody spoke a word, just dead silence, but I could hear all the fear in the silence, and I decided, right then and there, that I would make this silence my friend. People were beaten with clubs and whips for the smallest infractions. We weren't allowed to sit; people who sat were beaten. The Nazis allowed the Blockaltestes to whip and beat us for anything they might interpret as disobedience. Somehow, they knew who was sitting even when they were not there. We figured out later that they would look at the bottom of our dresses and beat the people who had dirt on them.

This seems obvious, but a lot of people were too sick and weak to stand. Red Cross vans were used to take the weak and sick to the gas chambers. A weapon was almost always used to inflict more pain. For some it took many beatings to get their point across.

When an SS man would beat you, he would use a club or a leather cat-o'-nine-tails to cause more damage. An SS touching one of us with his or her hands was considered beneath them, or contaminating, by his or her peers. There were so many things that put us in a state of disbelief that small bits of insane logic like this were hard to process. The world was so warped that to look at it with an eye for truth seemed tenuous at best.

People were dispatched to farms to cut and harvest wheat. Some people were marched into the woods to work on roads and clear brush. We stood there in line, for what seemed like hours, before we found out that we would be working that day. This was the morning routine for most of us. Once the counting was done, we were led to work by the labor commandos. That's when I heard strange music start playing. Recruited by the SS, a small group of prisoners were used to play military-style music. We were ordered to march to the beat of the music as we passed by and on our return. I'm sure that if they were playing for us back home, this is not the music they would have picked for us, but they were playing for their lives. I will tell you that many people never returned from these work details.

The usual working time amounted to eleven hours with a lunch break of half an hour. Lunch was served sometime after breakfast. We appreciated that small consistency. It was almost always a soup. There was so much hunger, and so little to concentrate the hunger upon, that we had names for each of the types of broth that we might get at lunch. The top part was the most watery. It contained very little of the starches from the vegetables in the pot. I no longer remember the name we gave it anymore, so I will now just call it "water broth." The middle was thicker and might contain pieces of vegetables. This was also the easiest to serve. The pot was still deep enough to dip the entire ladle into. The bottom part came with a price. Sure, there might be more actual pieces of vegetables, or on rare occasion, chicken, but there was usually also a layer of grit. Unwashed vegetables led to a film of dirt that sunk to the bottom of the mixture. This could be hard to digest, and even worse, it could create diarrhea. Bits of stones were hard to eat around and made the bottom of the pot always a danger.

The people in the camp were always starving, starving like nothing a modern person of means could ever imagine, starving like I would dream of filling my stomach just once more before I died. We all woke up starving. Dinner was a piece of bread and maybe some salami.

There were some women who had gone a little crazy. Those women would talk about the moment they received the food all day. They relived the size and shape of their meals: "It was thinner at one end than the other. I bet I get the next piece for dinner. It will be thicker at the other end, and they will fit together in my stomach. It will be beautiful." I actually don't know if those women were crazy or not. It just seemed very odd to me at the time how these women could talk about nothing.

But I found out quickly that at Auschwitz, people needed their denial to help them survive. For some, the truth could get them killed. To my sisters and me, there was a very deliberate message being delivered to us from the SS through these meager rations, or lack of them. This heartless food ritual was intended to slowly destroy us, and we felt it.

But maybe those women were the smart ones. Maybe they were only really living in the moment in the camp three times a day. And each of those slivers of life fed them until the next one came around.

The point is that the SS had to attempt to justify and create what their propaganda declared about us by reducing us to living at the lowest common denominator. When you beat, starve, murder, and dehumanize human beings, how could you expect sanity or common sense? The uglier they could make us, the easier it was for them to continue on with their deadly process. The truth is we were just ordinary people living normal lives. The mistake was those people who decided to listen to Hitler.

The first day came to a close, and I saw the terrible girl from the morning. She remembered me and pointed at the smokestack again. I couldn't tell if she was being horrible or helpful. I never got to find out. She was taken away and beaten the next day for being the next one in line behind someone who had stolen food from the kitchen. The guard was angry when he found the contraband. She had been made an example of, and the next day, she wasn't in our lineup, and I never saw her again.

As we entered the barracks to sleep that night, my sister Hedy was beaten by one of the SS. She had stopped to ask a question about the next day. The SS had a braided leather strap. It was like the ones we would later put together in the textile factory, in the town nearby, except hers was longer, and it snapped on the flesh with a crack, and then a sharp intake of breath immediately followed. She was hit again for questioning her beating. Then she was silent. We all were silent.

As the days and weeks passed, we slowly realized that this would be the extent of our daily lives from now on—lives set up by the SS for our eventual extermination. When we're

young and free, we have the cherished feeling we will live forever. This feeling was systematically stripped away by the SS.
To them, our lives were of no value, and it was their responsibility, as a courtesy, to rid society of that burden.

HEDY AND ROSE

Life, in its infinite wisdom, can trick you with lessons, and in some cases, extreme lessons. My two sisters Hedy and Rose experienced such personal transformations at Auschwitz that bonded them so completely as sisters. It made their relationship unshakable, everlasting, and eternal. What grew out of a petty, childish resentment awakened both of them to a reality of love, genuineness, and dependability for each other.

Back home, just before the war, Hedy and Rose's relationship became strained. In those days, there were no ready-made dresses. Everything was made by hand or by a dressmaker. My sisters and I were truly into fashion, especially Hedy, who was so beautiful and quite the free spirit. We were fortunate enough to have had our own dressmaker, named Gita, who made most of our clothes in her shop. One summer, she designed Rose a beautiful red dress, using fabric that Rose had specially handpicked. The dress was the latest fashion, with a beautiful matching jacket. Rose was so proud of her new dress; she modeled it for us all when she brought it home. She wanted to save it to wear for a special occasion, so she put it away in her closet until that day came. As sisters, we often shared clothes, but until Rose could wear it first, her new dress was off-limits.

One of our favorite things to do was to go to the park where the men would greet the ladies. We had lots of fun and always got so much attention. Hedy couldn't stop thinking about how beautiful she would look in Rose's dress. She knew wearing it would definitely increase her compliments. She decided foolishly to borrow it for herself. So one day, without Rose's permission, Hedy decorated herself in Rose's new dress. She eagerly headed to town, expecting the best outcome. Like I had mentioned earlier, the park was located near Piata Mare (Large Square), which was in the center of town. Most days, it was bustling with people. As Hedy strolled carefree through town, she began to walk toward the park. She did not notice that Rose was walking in her direction because she didn't know Rose had decided to do some shopping earlier. Before she could disappear or come up with a plan of explanation, it was too late, and Rose was right on top of her. Seeing that Hedy was wearing her new dress, the dress she had never worn, Rose was furious. She marched up to Hedy and demanded she go home immediately and take off her dress. The dress was tailor-made, and Hedy was just bit larger than Rose, which infuriated her; now her dress would be used, stretched and out of shape, not to mention she took it without asking.

Caught by her older sister, her plans and her day were now ruined completely. Hedy went home, humiliated.

Although this is a cute story, it created a serious wedge between my two sisters that caused Rose to stay upset for a very long time. A trust was broken with her that would not be completely healed until our arrival at Auschwitz. The healing wasn't something that my sisters had to sit down and talk about; after all, there were plenty of times they could have done that and didn't do so. Their wanting to control their previous falling-out paled in comparison to the circumstances in which they now found themselves. The luxury of time had vanished, and a sense of urgency took charge that would dissolve their petty differences completely, exposing the true depth of their relationship as sisters. What meant so much to us all before Auschwitz had no importance to us now whatsoever. The evil force, the well-oiled machine the SS called the Final Solution, was dedicated to the destruction of Jews but had a reverse outcome in my sisters, and they became one. While our mother and father were now gone, their voices grew from deep inside Hedy and Rose and gave them a quiet inner strength that I would desperately need to call on in the near future.

Any free time we had was usually at night after returning from work or after evening roll call. People visited among one another, trading things, fixing clothes, anything to try to improve our living conditions. There were all kinds of people from all walks of life: doctors, lawyers, teachers, students, artists, writers, poets, wealthy people, and poor people. People were from the occupied German territories Poland,

Czechoslovakia, Ukraine, Russia, my country, Hungary, and many more. Sometimes roll call could last for hours while people were disciplined for petty offenses. During the little free time we had, I tried to relax with my sisters. We would talk about the great food we had back home. Rose would even make herself dream about eating food when she went to sleep. She said that it worked; it helped her to not be so hungry when she woke up.

A lot of people concealed their talents out of fear of the SS tyranny. You didn't know what could get you killed. An offensive occupation could at best get you constantly ridiculed. There was a small underground of people who used their skills to barter for extra food and warm clothes. Some people discovered talents they didn't know they had.

My sisters and I often talked of our older brother Joseph, who was a brilliant salesman. We would say, "If Joseph were here, he would have taken charge and would have been a great service." Anything that we could smuggle in, we used up quickly, but sometimes people hung on to things such as food, extra clothing, and writing material to trade later.

Of course, the SS loved doing random searches and were always so proud when they found someone's little extra supply. They would be proud that they took away a small piece of food that could mean the life or death for that individual. If you were caught with something, you could be sure you would be beaten.

There was a charming woman from my hometown of Sighet who sang opera beautifully. She always seemed to smile at me when she looked my way. I felt her warmth and her strong desire to lift our spirits. When she sang, we all stopped what we were doing to listen to her. Her voice was so beautiful that it gave us all a momentary escape. For me, it was a small ray of sunlight shooting through the horror and darkness of Auschwitz. One night, right in the middle of a grand performance, a German guard who was outside of the barracks heard her singing and walked inside to see who it was. We all panicked for her. The guard kept silent and listened while she sang. After finishing her song, everyone in the barracks was completely still. Nobody dared to move or speak. We all waited anxiously to see what would happen. The guard approached the woman and said he had enjoyed her singing very much. He wanted her to sing for the SS officers, so he took her away with him. This was an audition for her life. We were so used to people being taken away at Auschwitz and never seeing them again.

We were all relieved when she returned. She sang for the SS officers, and they liked her so much that she was given a job to sing for them. Unfortunately, and I'm not sure what happened, but I found out later she didn't make it out of Auschwitz. I was only told that she was killed.

One day, I got separated from Hedy and Rose and was assigned to a work detail. This was the first time we had been separated since we arrived at Auschwitz. I was afraid and could see my sisters were very worried.

They said, "Don't worry, Klara. You will be okay."

After roll call, we marched through the camp and made our way past the orchestra in a single-file line. I don't remember how far it was or how long we walked, but it seemed like forever. SS guards with dogs escorted us. We must have walked a few miles when we stopped at a field. It was a field of cut wheat, and our job was to tie and knot the wheat into small bundles.

I was so clumsy, and this was so different to me. I had no idea how to tie a proper knot. There were guards everywhere with barking dogs. We were put into groups and shown how to make the bundles.

One guard noticed I wasn't making the knot tight enough and became angry. The guard yelled, *"Versagerin!"* which means "failure." He hit me with his club all over my body. Then, there were two and three guards around me with their dogs, and they yelled, *"Versagerin! Versagerin!"* The dogs growled and barked, and it scared me when they came within inches of biting me.

When the guard finally stopped hitting me, I was in tremendous pain. I looked around at the other women for some kind of support, but their heads were all down in fear that they would be next. The bundles were not that difficult to make. I made them correctly after the beating, making the knots tight. Being the first day in the field, I believe the guard was making an example of me. He needed to set the tone for what we could expect if we weren't absolutely flawless in following orders. I was bruised all over my body for about two weeks, but with Hedy and Rose's help, my wounds healed. I began to slowly make my way and adjust to the Auschwitz routine.

SEPARATED FROM ROSE

Unfortunately, at Auschwitz, although there were acts of heroism and acts of kindness, there was also plenty of treachery and selfishness. Families fought over scraps of food, possessions, and clothing. Fortunately for me, my two sisters were my selfless heroes.

Hedy and I had gotten separated from Rose because we had both developed a rash. We were taken to what they called an infirmary until it cleared up so we wouldn't infect the others. Actually, it wasn't an infirmary or hospital at all. It was just a small room for quarantine. We were all made to stay there until we healed. Food had become very lean, and the portions were meager at best. Rose was able to get an extra small piece of salami from God knows where. She refused to eat that piece of salami without us and risked making her way over to the infirmary. She found a small open window and called to us. She demanded that we share it with her. I don't think it was about the salami. Rose said she was desperate to see her two sisters. She needed to know we were alive and all right. That's when I realized how great my family was. We were all dying, and yet, because of that constant threat, we were forced to grow up. It was at that moment that I knew my two sisters' past wounds and differences had completely healed. Hedy and Rose had become the two sisters that I always dreamed they could be.

Of course, at Auschwitz, you could never ever feel safe or secure. I did begin to discover the who, what, and wheres that would be more of a threat to our survival. Even knowing that, at Auschwitz, there were no guarantees. We could never trust our block leader, Lilly, who watched over us with her older sister. Lilly was brutal and mean, and although she wasn't Jewish, she was a prisoner with us from Czechoslovakia. Lilly was a cruel representative working for the SS and thought of herself only.

SELECTED BY DR. JOSEF MENGELE

Looking back, there were things that I couldn't have known then that stand out to me now. For instance, some circumstances and events seemed to command more of my attention than others. Transports arrived daily but departed daily too. Once again we were ordered to stand in line. Factory owners from other camps across Europe would send in request orders for women to work slave labor jobs for the German war effort. The SS would do full body inspections on us in the nude and pick women to go to these factories who they felt were the best fit. As one transport would leave, another would arrive. I can remember being fixated on the women going to the bathhouse. From there, they would leave on transports to other camps. At the same time these transports were leaving, the big generators would fire up the crematoriums, which signaled new transports would soon arrive at Auschwitz. I often wondered if the

German factory owners had any knowledge of what was happening. Did they know the trains that were bringing them their new workers had been used to transport thousands of people to their deaths? Did they know about the mass murders taking place at Auschwitz?

We were told to always look down at the floor and never to look in Mengele's eyes. Mengele looked for any reason to put people to death. He loved the power that came with being able to decide who lived and who died. Mengele made regular visits to our barracks and other women's barracks He was always accompanied by armed guards along with a phony smile and hidden agenda. By now, all of the women were terrified of him because we never knew when he would appear. If and when he did show up, someone was usually selected for torture or escorted to the gas chambers because they appeared sick or malnourished.

If politics, culture, or religion weren't expedient, Mengele would turn to science or even medicine. An infected Jew might infect more Jews, or by some tragedy, the disease might unwittingly infect a so-called *real* person. A German might die because of a Jew who was sick. I believe that was why he so quickly dealt with any outbreaks of sickness in the camp. I never saw any regard or compassion for the lives of those living within Auschwitz. The sick were abandoned quickly. This is another example of how the Jews were disposed of and abandoned. During my second month in the camp, someone came down with typhoid fever in the neighboring barracks. Mengele's mission to stop the epidemic was extreme.

The next day, the barracks was completely empty. Mengele ordered seven hundred women to the gas chambers that night because of one case of typhoid.

Mengele sent whole barracks to the gas chambers over thirty times during his reign at Auschwitz. Sometimes one barracks, sometimes an entire section of the camp was completely emptied overnight. This was something that the block leaders helped the SS control. At first, I thought this was strange. Then I realized that the block leaders were relatively safe from Mengele's spot selections. They had jobs in the intake centers, which meant they could sneak clothing and steal food to keep themselves healthy and comfortable. However, Josef Mengele would kill anyone if he thought she was sick, no matter what job she had. The one thing the block leaders could not escape was his order for their execution.

These constant reminders of the camp affected everyone differently. My mind was always drawn toward the new transports that arrived, which were at least two per day. My sisters and I felt obligated to gently explain to the new arrivals in our barracks that part of their family, if not all, was gone. Rose, being the oldest, usually did most of the talking. Hedy and I sat with her for support. This was always painful, but necessary for their well-being if they were going to have any chance of surviving. It's also what our mother and father would have wanted us to do. Of course, our reassuring them didn't always work. Some people gave up because the loss was too overwhelming.

People committed suicide, sometimes by running and throwing themselves up against the electric fence, which was always lethal. Thankfully, I never had to see that happen. I only heard about it afterward. It was devastating enough finding out that people you had tried to help had killed themselves. My pain and my loss started all over again, which left me empty and hopeless. It became a circle of sadness beyond description, all of which was orchestrated by the SS.

After about three months at the camp, I began to get sick, though my sickness was strange. It was partly in my body and partly in my mind. Days of hard work in the fields surrounding the camp were piled upon days of watching people shoveled into the factory of death, and my mind, as well as my body, began to break down. The expressions on the newcomers' faces, their horror of the revelation of the true nature of the camp had become normal, but it wasn't the kind of normal that I could live with in my mind.

I had been moved from working in the field to a textile factory, which started every morning at five o'clock. We were assigned to put together pieces of clothing to keep others warm. It was freezing. I saw a girl, younger than me, being beaten out of the corner of my eye. That's when I noticed that the corner of my eye had seen too much. That was the day that I stopped eating completely, but I continued to work. The bread they gave us at night only seemed like a means to prolong our existence. I tried to give it to my sisters, but they refused and begged me to eat.

As my body deteriorated, I became less sensitive to the world around me. I stopped listening to Hedy and Rose, who would beg me constantly, "Klara, Klara, please eat!" I knew how terribly concerned they were, but I simply couldn't eat. I stopped feeling the cold, and I could feel my mind slipping into darkness, into a place that I had seen so many others fall.

Things seemed to be moving quicker in the camp as the SS scurried around. Rumors flew that the war, for Germany, was lost. I thought that the music we heard as we marched that day was the last music I would hear in my life. A violin's string stretched to the point of breaking. Hands were pushing on it, and a bow sawed back and forth. It shrieked. I felt that was me. When we marched back after our work detail, the barracks were silent, and so was I. I had finished speaking forever.

Things that couldn't be revealed to me then are clearer to me now. Some things can be very difficult to describe, but I felt like I had become two people that split into multiple people and looked at layers and levels of things all at once. I realized that I wasn't merely one solid human being, and that we were more than that, and everything seemed to have paradoxical importance attached to it. People left on trains for a better place as fire and smoke released ashes from the chimneys of the crematorium. I could feel things were in motion, a movement that was moving me, my sisters, the war, Auschwitz, and all its players to its final conclusion. I knew the longer I stayed at Auschwitz, my past would get longer, but my future would get shorter. The day ended. It was my last day in Auschwitz.

It was November. A cold gray sky blocked out the sun. Mengele came out of his office and announced that there would be a selection in our barracks. Lilly ordered us to quickly prepare for a lineup. The crematorium had been burning day and night. The Germans knew that the Russian front was advancing and this was not good for them. They continually tried to get rid of the evidence of what they were doing. There was literally a holding block that held a backlog of people waiting for the gas chambers to clear so they could be gassed too. My sisters and I knew people waited sometimes days to be gassed, with no food or water. I think this frustrated Mengele. He couldn't simply send people directly to the gas chambers anymore, and it changed his routine. There was some slight satisfaction in that. When Mengele came to our barracks that day, we knew people were going to the gas chamber. Mengele marched inside, dressed in his white lab coat, which covered his uniform, with five big German guards in tow.

We were ordered to hold our dress, coat, or whatever we were wearing in our right hands; our left hands were to be empty. We had to be undressed, completely nude. We were to stay in a single-file line and walk toward him while he looked over our bodies. As the soldiers stood guard, Mengele methodically decided whom he would send to the gas chambers and whom he would send back to work. Mengele's decision to kill was always justified by a spot-check medical exam. But it wasn't medical at all; it was just another way he used to torture people. It was a psychological torture he used by holding everyone hostage before he decided whom he would kill.

I knew Hedy and Rose were very concerned that Mengele would pick me to go to the gas chamber, but there was nothing I could do anymore. I was very sick and had lost too much weight. Mengele had already selected about thirty women to die before he came to us. Fear gripped the room. Women cried for their loved ones as the guards separated the condemned from the others. Those who were selected quietly wept. My sisters put me in front of them because they felt maybe if I went before them, my skeletal frame might not be noticed. The closer we got to Mengele, I knew we were going to come face-to-face with the man who had murdered my family. We had been told to always look down and never look Mengele in the eyes. As we came closer, he let a few girls in front of me pass. Then it came time for me. I didn't look down; I looked straight into his eyes. I no longer cared or was afraid. I needed to look into the eyes of the man who had killed my family. Not that it mattered, Mengele was evil, and he wasn't going to let any act of defiance show that it affected him, especially coming from a young Jewish girl from Sighet. As he looked up and down my body, I knew in that moment I was selected. He put his hand out to stop me. His hand signal was an unspoken order for everyone in the barracks to halt.

He grabbed my left hand, looked at my number, and then with just a wave from his other hand, he pointed to one of the guards and said, *"Sieben, acht, vier, funf, ausschreiben,"* and then let my hand go. That means "Seven, eight, four, five, write it down." And with that, now it was official. I was selected and quickly escorted past Hedy and Rose.

There was no delay. I was taken with the others directly to the bathhouse. They gave me a black dress to wear. There was bleacher-like seating, and we were told to sit there and wait. The line of women kept pouring inside the room. Some women were crying, some were stunned, and some were hysterical. We all knew this was the end. There was nothing that could change our fate. We were completely innocent human beings. There would be no reprieve for the innocent, no last-minute stay of execution. We only had a few hours left to live, at best, and knew the end that was waiting for us. There were probably seventy or seventy-five women that Mengele had decided that he had no use for that day. They all looked so bad, so sick, and afraid. I knew I must look the same to them, but I still found a moment to pity them. The darkness closed in, and I wondered how long it would be. I kept staring at the bars on the window, thinking of Hedy and Rose. I could hear muffled weeping coming from different corners of the room. There were random wails from others. Some women just crawled into the corner and held themselves. I looked around, and I stayed silent.

MY ESCAPE

I thought to myself, *God knows how long we've been here and when this death camp will end. If the war keeps going much longer, they're going to kill us slowly anyway; we're all going to die. If the front comes forward, we're going to die before they arrive.* I figured, why suffer? It was better to die there and then than to live a life like this, as a prisoner.

There was a special name for girls who were as thin as me. We were called *Muselmann*, which means we were walking skeletons, like we were ready to drop dead at any moment. The body loses all shape that defines man or woman. I had recently grown into the body of a woman, and now I had lost it. We took our bodies for granted even then. I can't remember the change from puberty, not the way that it felt. I don't remember the way my body felt when I grew three inches over one summer. I do, however, remember the way my body felt that day. The feeling of skin hanging off of bone is one that is never forgotten.

I don't know how my sisters managed to make it to the building where we were held, but they did. They certainly risked their lives to be there. My sisters came to the bars at the window, crying and screaming out to me. They sounded like they were in horrible pain. It was as if they were dying, because for them, losing their little sister was like losing a part of themselves. My sisters and I knew how I was to be killed. There's a real emotional price to knowing that.

There was never time for my mother, father, or little brother, Mortho, to process death before it happened; that nearly drove my sisters insane.

"You'll be all right, Klara! Everything will be okay," they shouted over and over. I could hear them being beaten for coming too close to the building, but they wouldn't stop trying to comfort me.

I said nothing. I was like a stone. I couldn't find my voice to say, "Don't worry about me. I'm fine. I'm not scared to die. I'm going to be okay." I thought that I was better off, that they should kill me now rather than I suffer.

I heard Hedy and Rose's screams fade off into the distance as they were pulled away saying, "Klara, don't be afraid. Don't be afraid."

I wasn't afraid. I just didn't want to suffer anymore. In a way, it felt like I was giving up on myself entirely, but I wasn't giving up. I don't know exactly what happened, but I just let go. At that moment I completely surrendered to my fate. I became hyperalert. I felt my body moved by this surrender, a mystery that I can't explain. I don't know why, but I couldn't say a word to them. Maybe if they had only heard my voice it might have given them comfort. Why couldn't I do at least that? I have no answer to this day.

Sometime later, five big guards burst in and said they were moving us to a smaller building to wait in a room closer to the gas chambers. We had been tricked and lied to so much that no one knew what to believe. Were they really taking us somewhere else? Or were they taking us directly to the gas chamber? Was this it? The SS were masters of deception.

People began to pray out loud. I knew Hedy and Rose were unaware that I had been moved, and by now, they probably thought I was dead. It was still nighttime when the door flew open and we were once again escorted by armed guards outside. The light from the menacing flood lamps that lit up the camp from the guard towers pierced my eyes, momentarily blinding me. I reached out and grabbed the first person I could to keep my body moving forward and not stumble. We walked for a short period, until we came to a smaller brick-style building where we were shoved inside. Again, we were told to wait. A small bit of relief permeated the room. People gasped when they realized this wasn't the gas chamber but a small holding room next to it. But, I knew now, this was the end. The next door waiting for us, the next door we would go through would be the door entering the Auschwitz gas chamber.

When I set up the extermination building at Auschwitz, I used Zyklon-B, which was a crystallized prussic acid which we dropped into the death chamber from a small opening. It took from three to fifteen minutes to kill the people in the death chamber depending on climatic conditions. We knew when the people were dead because the screaming stopped. We usually waited about one half hour before we opened the doors and removed the bodies. After the bodies were removed, our special commandos took off the rings and extracted the gold from the teeth of the corpses. (Rudolf Hess, commandant of Auschwitz, testimony at Nuremberg, 1946)

After a few hours, the girls around me fell asleep from crying and exhaustion. As far as I could tell, except for the guards on the other side of the door that I couldn't see, I was the only one awake. I didn't cry, and I didn't fall asleep. Instead, I walked around the room. I couldn't stop thinking of my sisters. They were so upset. I felt like I had to let them know that I was okay. I thought to myself, what could I do to get out of here?

I kept looking at the door, waiting for something to change, but it never did. Everything was perfectly still. The two guards were ready to stop anyone who came too close.

I walked around and touched the walls. They were made of bricks, but not real bricks. They were the inferior kinds that were more dirt or adobe (earth and straw) than cement. Yes, I knew bricks from the days in my family's dry goods business. I found a window out of view of the door, with bars, and I pushed on one of the bricks to see if I could get it to move. It didn't budge. I tried another, but again, nothing. Then I noticed that there were marks where it looked like another prisoner had dug around the bottom of one of the bricks. My hands shook, but I pushed and pulled at that brick.

I switched to rocking it back and forth, and it started to move. Once it was free, I used it to chip at the others. It took no time at all. The other bricks just pulled out, one after another. It was such a small passage, but my slender body slid under the iron, and I scrambled through the space, into the night.

I had escaped! I felt the fresh, cold air and a release from the horror. I wanted to live now, with all my heart. The freedom was so quick, so sudden, and so new that I forgot about dying. In a way, I had already died, so moving forward became the only option. I was still in the middle of the prison camp, and I still had an ordered death sentence from Mengele. They had my number. They had written it down. It was only a matter of time before they put me back into that room.

What I wanted to do most, I couldn't. I wanted to join my sisters and let them know that I had found a way out. The block leaders would recognize me, and then all of this would have been for nothing.

It was so cold. I still remember the wet, snowy rain as it fell onto my skin. The night made buildings into coal tracings.

Light from spotlights crossed overhead. I crouched and I thought in the dark. I knew I needed to get out of the dress that marked me for death. I knew that the intake center was one of the few places where a person could steal clothing, but that would be too risky. I stayed close to the buildings away from the open grounds. The guards were less consistent in the winter. Nobody wanted to be outside, even those with warm winter jackets and long underwear. I was in a thin cotton dress, slipping through the frigid winter wind.

I could see there were lights on in the bathhouse. A thick layer of steam covered the inside of the windows. I remember wiping the window with my hand, but of course, the steam was on the other side. I can remember that with a little amusement. If girls were in the showers at this time, I might be lucky. They may be sending a group to another camp. We knew that trains had been leaving regularly. As the Russian front approached, the SS were shipping the "useful" Jews farther into the country to help with the German war effort.

If this was a work transport I wasn't picked to go on, I would be exposed. I had been picked to die. I knew my only hope was to escape. The bitter cold cut through me like thousands of knives. I couldn't last long in that weather. I needed to get inside and maybe onto one of the trains. It was deathly quiet as I slid along the side of the bathhouse wall. And then, like a miracle, I came to a window of the bathhouse that had no glass, no bars, no covering at all, just a square hole. I quickly climbed inside.

All of the steam in the room helped to cover me so I could easily integrate with the others. But there was little time; I needed to quickly get oriented.

I dropped my dress and walked into the showers. I tried not to look at anyone. For once, the atmosphere of intimidation and degradation worked to my favor. Nobody looked at me. We stepped out of the showers, and we were given dresses and shoes. I learned that the Germans were sending one hundred girls to a camp in Czechoslovakia. I pushed my way forward. I was in the second or third line of girls. We stood in the frigid cold and waited to be counted.

The SS were notorious counters. They treated numbers like a religion. There was to be five to a line and twenty lines. Then, the sergeant who was counting us came to the end. It was a staggering thing for him. It made no sense at all. He counted to 101, not 100.

They took the girl at the end and dragged her back toward the bathhouse. She was upset. She cried out, "Why are you going to take me away? I was selected to go with the transport."

Number 101 protested and was pulled backward into that terrible place. There was definitely responsibility on my shoulders. Was I being selfish? Should I have simply come forward right then and said that I was really the 101st girl in this transport? I would like to say that I had these questions and answers at the time, but I can't recall feeling anything but cold and afraid and thinking, *Just hold on and stay quiet for a little longer.* I could see my own breath while others stood waiting in the freezing cold night for the answer to come.

Like a salvation, a girl from the middle of the group called out, "Let me stay! I don't want to go. I want to stay with my family." She had her number on the list marked for deportation.

I could hear a short discussion among the guards. "How long do you want to stand out here in the cold?"

"This is the list?"

"Do you want to go recount and hold everything up?"

My heart pounded as we all waited. I had done everything I could. I had broken all the Auschwitz rules to get this far and now time stood still.

Then, I heard the sergeant make his decision to take the girl who wanted to stay back to her barracks. "Put this one back in line! Load the train! *Schnell!*" Then I felt a surge in the line and heard again *"Schnell! Schnell!"* ("Quickly! Quickly!")

The lines moved toward the open doors of the cargo train. Line after line was loaded. This time, there were fewer girls in each car. The car began to warm up as more bodies filled it. I don't know why some people live and why some people die, but when people are liberated from a very deadly situation, there is a mystery that we neglect to embrace. I was chosen to die in the gas chambers at Auschwitz by Mengele, but something greater than the both of us decided otherwise. All I can tell you is what happened, but I can't tell you why it happened.

The train cars were loaded, and the doors slammed shut. I was in the dark again. I had food in my hands. They had given us a whole loaf of bread and a big piece of salami. I had a new dress on my back. We were traveling, against all odds, away from Auschwitz, and for whatever reason, and no matter what happened, from this point on, it would seem we were all free—at least from that tyranny.

The train moved into the night. It turned out that it wasn't only the body heat that made me feel warm. A fever was coming over me. I still couldn't eat, so I sat there with the bread in my hands, like a statue. My wasted body could not sleep. The farther we traveled from Auschwitz, the more human we became. People began to move around the car. I began to feel like an outsider as I felt all eyes examine me.

Next, I heard a voice say to the others, "What is that Muselmann doing here?"

A tall girl with a tuft of gray hair startled me from behind. She spoke about me in disgust, like I was not human. I guess we were not far enough from Auschwitz yet.

I moved away from her. My joints crackled from being in the same position all night. Sweat soaked my dress. I could see others assessing my condition, and moved away. My body was falling apart. They had all seen it before. I had bread and meat, uneaten from the night before, which was desirable. I was safe from Auschwitz but not safe from the system of inhumanity. At that moment, I understood I still couldn't let my guard down. The bread and meat gave me some value and a modest advantage.

One of the girls followed me to a dark corner. "Are you going to eat those?" She spoke in soft tones. It was like she was afraid I might bite her.

"Maybe," I said in a voice that was dry and weak. I could see that the girl was deciding whether she should offer me something for the food or just wait until I died. I didn't think she had anything I wanted, so it didn't really concern me much. I didn't want to talk to her anymore anyway.

"I have some sugar," the girl said.

My reaction was immediate. I thrust the bread and salami into her hands. I didn't even wait to find out how much I would get. I just wanted a taste of something sweet. I wanted it to dissolve on my tongue so I wouldn't have to swallow. My stomach was probably the size of an acorn by that time.

"Give it to me, please," I whispered. It was strange to want something after so much time. I cherished that sugar like a child. I licked my hand, and then I let the feeling wash over me. I waited, sometimes hours, before I would lick it again. Each time, it felt like I must have finished it, but each time I came back and found more in the pit of my hand.

We traveled for three days and three nights. It took so long because we would make stops or be routed off of the track so more important shipments could go through unimpeded. It felt like we were stationary almost as much as we were in motion. Our transport was full of able-bodied girls, but I saw the heartbreak in their eyes. They all had their own personal stories; their tragedy was their own. It lived on them like some haunting spirit that no amount of makeup or beautiful clothes or anything like that could hide. I wondered how I must look. I could feel myself rapidly worsening and my sickness advancing. At times, I was disoriented to the point where I didn't really know where I was. I must have begun speaking to myself, because I heard my voice in the darkness when everyone was asleep. I had no idea where we were going. I knew that we were going somewhere else, but I had no idea where.

Finally, the powerful engines of the train slowed to a stop. My body could hardly feel the weight and heartbeat of the train as we sat in silence, anticipating the unknown, powerless. Would it be different this time? We had all been in this situation before.

The doors flew open, and a captain barked in German, "Five to a line!"

Not much seemed different. They counted us. They moved us to the gates, and then I felt it: I could go no further. I couldn't march in one more line. My mind would have no more, and I no longer cared what happened next. My body finally gave out. I collapsed, and the next two weeks of my story have been pieced together only from the account of a woman, a Jewish doctor, that tended over me in the infirmary. I didn't feel human. I had come from a place where people shouldn't get too close to the sick or those too far gone.

HUMANITY

Weisswasser, Czechoslovakia, was a small town located near the Polish border. Even though the war had turned badly for the Nazis, they still occupied parts of Czechoslovakia and were putting up strong resistance all across Europe. Weisswasser was purely a Nazi slave labor camp. Jewish women from Hungary, Poland, Romania, and France were transported from Auschwitz to work at privately owned factories. Prisoners worked for a company named Telefunken. During the Second World War, Telefunken was a supplier of vacuum tubes, transmitters, and radio relay systems. They developed radar facilities and directional finders, aiding extensively the German air defense against British-American aerial bombing.

∞∞∞

Survival hardly feels like heroism, especially when all it took was a glance from a soldier in the camp or a policeman in the streets and I could be shot dead or sentenced to death.

I woke up very disoriented in a hospital bed in the infirmary. I can only tell someone who hasn't had to sleep in the conditions of Auschwitz that waking up alive and in a bed was like a glass of the finest wine for the body and soul. I was still frail, sick, and my organs were on the cusp of systemic failure, but I was in a real bed. There were at least ten to twenty beds in the Weisswasser infirmary. People were sent to the infirmary for everything from minor complaints to serious disorders. It always seemed to be full. Even though the people who came here got well, the hospital had limited supplies and only the necessary medical provisions. There was no IV therapy at Weisswasser, just liquids and a starchy broth that I gratefully drank. I had a fever, and it was causing me to pass in and out of consciousness. My memory was sketchy at best for the first few weeks, so my first visit with my savior felt a little strange. I believe having a female doctor was what I needed at the time, and the fact that she was Jewish, too, was of great help in my recovery.

"You need to eat. If you eat, you can leave, and I can have the bed," she said.

"My name is Klara." It was the only thing I could think to say.

She touched my hand and made me comfortable. She wanted to know where I was from, and I told her Sighet. She smiled and told me that she was from Czechoslovakia.

She had beautiful long black hair and looked about forty years old, but she was probably in her late twenties or thirties. The war aged some people beyond their years, sometimes dramatically. Younger people seemed to manage a little better. I was seventeen, but she probably thought I was twelve or thirteen. My face had been sculpted back to the bone, gaunt and chalk white. I was a ghost. This weakness and frailty turned me into more of a child in the eyes of those at the camp. The doctor could have easily carried me like a child. And it very well might have been necessary since I was sometimes not conscious enough to even walk.

I weighed about the same as your average eight-year-old boy. That was my condition. The infirmary doctor was very gentle with me physically and with her bedside manner. She took to me like I was her daughter.

"Klara, you are a good girl, you know," she told me one day. She said I was very critical and not out of the woods yet. I still didn't feel well. I still felt weak. I said nothing. She then said, "You are brave, I can tell."

Although I didn't fully believe that either, I said, "Thank you."

She smiled and kindly kidded me, saying, "Be careful, Klara. We're almost having a conversation." Her eyes were so bright. There was so much intelligence and kindness behind them. I don't remember anyone ever calling her by her name; they only referred to her as Doctor. Yet there is no one more responsible for my recovery and who I am today than she.

The days passed quickly. I was in the infirmary for a total of six weeks. Women came in and out of the other beds. Some of them had heard of me. I thought that one woman who came to the infirmary had been with me on the train from Auschwitz. She seemed happy to see me when she saw me lying in the bed. I knew now that we were far away from Auschwitz. She talked to me. I didn't really understand what she was saying, and her Hungarian was broken, so I thought that she might be asking a question. Was I dreaming? I didn't know what to say. I still remember her face. She must have remembered when I fainted after I stepped off of the train. I slept that night, and for the next week or so, I drifted in and out of dreams and thoughts.

I wanted to leave several times, but the doctor always said, "Klara, no, you are not ready." It took a while for her to get control of my fever.

Finally, after about six weeks, I woke up to the smell of coffee and powdered eggs. I walked to the doctors' station. "I am ready to leave," I said.

The doctor replied, "See, I told you that you were brave. None of these other girls have volunteered to go back to work." Her voice was stern, but again there was a gentle smile on her lips.

She spoke about me with the German captain when he came in that day. She used the same tone that she did with us. Her voice was powerful and direct. Although the words she used represented a request, it was not a question. She wanted me to work in a position where I would not be stressed. She told the captain that I was a good girl and that I should be treated well.

A woman, a Jewish woman, was telling a captain in the German army what to do? To my astonishment, he followed her request. I reported to my job the next day. The factory in town manufactured radio systems that were privately owned by the Telefunken Company. The owners of this company needed us all healthy and fit so we could work efficiently. I was told by one of the girls that the owners of the factory made plenty of money through our free labor. We were lined up and counted before we were marched to the factory. I was shown to my station, which was a round table with about six to eight women sitting around it. I learned to put wire transmitters and radio relay systems together. It was a strange transition. I'd been afraid. I'd been hungry. I'd been beaten and bruised, but there hadn't been a single moment during the war, until that factory, where I had been bored. I was wonderfully and restfully bored. I fell asleep at my job.

It took some time, but I began to eat regular meals. Eating was painful at first. It was like building new muscles. The strain of starting the process of digestion again stretched at my insides. Hot foods felt like they seared through me, and cold foods felt like they sat in my stomach like a stone. The food tasted much better, and there was more of it. We were given three meals a day, and each of them included bread and meat.

The Germans who ordered us into lines wore green uniforms; actually it was a green-gray color. They had not been trained by the SS, who wore the infamous black uniform. Maybe it was because they knew the end was coming, but by the time that I got there, they were treating the prisoners like prisoners and not like cattle. I heard from one of the women at the camp that there had been brutal guards in the past, but, for the most part, they were not there anymore. For once, things were good, and we all had a lot of time to reflect and think. We twisted wires and fused caps onto them. I considered the idea that brutality was part of the way to rise in the chain of command in the SS. Perhaps all of these SS guards, the ones who wanted to kill without conscience, had been moved to where they could kill more effectively. Every day, the whole process got clearer for me, and my experience began to unravel. This ugly side of humanity had started long ago, beginning with the anti-Semitism we experienced in Sighet to the taking away of our rights and our possessions, followed by the ghetto roundups, and then, finally being deported to Auschwitz.

Now I was at a different kind of camp—a slave labor camp, or a business camp, if you will—designed cheaply to help the German war machine while bringing huge profits to the factory owners. Each time I drifted off to sleep, my thoughts went back to Auschwitz. If only I could have said something to my sisters before I left. My failure was hopelessly tied to my inability to comfort them or put them at ease.

Many trains came from Auschwitz while I was working at Weisswasser. I thought if I could get on the detail that met each one, I could check the new arrivals for my sisters, if they were ever sent here. Subsequently, the trains no longer came from Auschwitz. Whatever my sisters' story was, I was not going to be able to hear it here; that chapter was over.

I'm not certain, but it might have been two months until my own liberation. It's hard to call it that because it did not happen like anything I had seen in the movies. There were very few heroes in the war; more often, the villains changed as power changed hands. I just wanted to see Hedy and Rose again. I wanted to say one thing to them, and then I'd be fine with whatever came next. I'd already let them down once, and I could not fail again.

Even though trains were not arriving from Auschwitz, they did arrive infrequently from other camps. Each day I still held out hope that I would see Hedy and Rose come into Weisswasser. They had each other, and they both were fairly healthy when I was taken away. I wanted them to see me as much as I wanted to see them.

The supply lines to the factory became less regular. There were days when we did not have the necessary raw materials to run the line. On those days, they still sat us in our positions at the table, but nothing happened. It was like some silent movie set with someone waiting to call, "Action!" Nothing moved; nobody spoke. The whistle blew at five, and we marched back to our barracks.

Then, one day, something amazing happened. It was early morning, and we lined up in the yard with our packs and waited to be counted. Then, we were taken to the factory. When we arrived at the factory, we waited and waited, but nobody came. It felt like some kind of trick.

We must have waited an hour before the woman who took care of us went up to the quarters that the Germans kept in a loft above us. She came back with a look of astonishment on her face.

With an uncertainty to her voice, she said, "It's empty. They're gone."

And then a girl said, "What does this mean? Are there no more orders? Are we free?"

The Germans had run away. I looked around, and there were no guards or German soldiers anywhere. Suddenly, it was like all of the energy that we kept inside us was released, and the first thing that came out was laughter. We all started to laugh. Other women screamed and cried. The whole thing was hysterical. And it was something beautiful, another scene I will never forget. Little by little, we scattered about and enjoyed the moment. Now, we could freely loiter about without anyone coming to give an order or to punish us. Dreams of a new life were rarely talked about, but everybody had them hidden deep within their hearts. As we started to settle down, you could hear all of the dreams and plans of the other women surface to the top in anticipation of this day's arrival.

A new journey had just begun for all of us. And the strange thing was, we didn't run for the doors. It took us some time to trust this new development, and we were very cautious. The courage to walk out of the camp came gradually. I don't know about the others, but I realized that Weisswasser and its routine had, ironically, become a place of safety for me.

When I walked out of the front gate of Weisswasser, I walked about thirty feet and stopped. I looked back and thought, *Is this true? Nobody is following me, I'm free? I can walk away? It's okay?* And it dawned on me. *I* am *free!*

MENGELE ON THE RUN

On January 27, 1945, at 3:00 p.m., the Russian army entered the gates of Auschwitz-Birkenau, liberating the Auschwitz death camp. The Nazis retreated to Germany months later, overpowered and beaten by Allied forces as the Russians advanced from the east.

Just ten days earlier, Dr. Josef Mengele, aware of Germany's inevitable defeat, plotted his escape, left Auschwitz, and began his life as a fugitive where he would master avoiding capture by the Allies. Although Mengele was in custody on different occasions, through fate or well-rehearsed manipulation, he managed to elude every effort to hold him accountable for his war crimes. In April of 1945, Mengele was named as a leading war criminal by the International War Tribunal.

Forced to be constantly on the move, Mengele was always afraid of being captured by Israeli intelligence agents and suffering the same fate as Adolf Eichmann, who was caught, sent back to Israel, tried for war crimes, and executed. Mengele, who was once the commander of life and death at Auschwitz, was now a marked man.

Discovered in letters to his son, Rolf, and his own personal diaries, Mengele continued to be dedicated to his racist views and expressed no remorse for his atrocities. With help from family, and sheltered by Nazi sympathizers, for over thirty years, Mengele cleverly managed to sidestep punishment for his horrific crimes. Later confirmed by DNA analysis, it is believed he died on February 7, 1979, on a beach at Bertioga, in Embu, Brazil, having suffered a stroke while swimming in the ocean. In just under two years, Mengele was personally responsible for the murder and torture of tens of thousands of human beings. As many as two thousand people a day were sent to the gas chambers at Auschwitz.

On May 7, 1945, with Germany in shambles, they surrender. On May 8, World War II, in Europe, is over.

THE JOURNEY HOME

As evening fell, most of us decided to go back into the camp of Weisswasser to spend the night. To get back home would be a very long journey for all of us, and we wanted to start out in daylight. Some people decided to leave that day on their own. The Allies had bombed the trains throughout Europe, and in our area, they were completely destroyed. Sighet was a few thousand miles from Weisswasser, and I had no idea if I would even be able to find an operating train. We all needed food and a plan before we began our journeys.

The next day, the Russians arrived.

To my surprise, the Russian captain who led his men was Jewish. We immediately surrounded him with our requests. He was bombarded by twenty to thirty Jewish women who wanted food and to go home. I could tell he was a good man. Being a good man and Jewish, what else could he do but help us?

Only one woman spoke Russian, and through her interpretation and our desperation, the captain calmly came up with a plan. He lit his cigarette and said, "The train tracks headed south are completely destroyed. You won't get to your homes by train." He paused. "Here's how I can help you. I will give a letter of passage to a Czechoslovakian gentleman who I know. He owns a large truck. The letter will state that his truck is not to be confiscated by the Russian army."

The Russian girl spoke up and asked, "What if he refuses your request?"

"I will confiscate his truck and send it to Russia if he refuses," said the captain. "I will arrange for this man to pick up as many women as he can and take them south to the nearest operating trains, however far that may be. I believe the nearest is a two-day journey from here. Take as many food supplies from the camp as you can. It's not much, but that's the best I can do. Good luck making your way home."

We were instructed to be ready within a few hours to leave Weisswasser—forever.

I'd never ridden in the back of a large truck with thirty women before. It didn't matter that we were crowded; we were so happy, and excited to be alive and going home. The rough ride was minor in comparison to what we had endured. Everything had changed overnight. We were free! There was a lot of laughter. I could feel an awakening occurring. Everything was fresh and brand-new.

After a long day on the road, we came to a small town and spent the night in a schoolhouse. There were women from all of the different camps staying there as they searched for ways to get to their homes. Our truck was full, and as we were preparing to leave the next day, I ran into a girl in the school yard. The girl wouldn't let me pass. She was unusually excited, and she couldn't speak for a moment.

Finally, she asked, "Where are you from?"

Before answering her, I thought it was a trick, so I asked, "Do I know you...Where are you from?" The skin around the girl's eyes was swollen, and she looked a sickly shade of white. I didn't trust her.

"I am from Sighet," she said. She didn't look like anyone I knew from my town. It wasn't a big town, but I knew most everyone and thought I'd never seen her before. Then she said, "I'm Rabbi Aizckson's wife. My name is Hanolo."

I remembered the girl she was talking about. She was beautiful and elegant and considered a socialite. Her husband, Rabbi Aizckson, was a famous rabbi in Sighet. And now, this person standing in front of me bore practically no resemblance to my memory. She talked about the town, my sisters and brothers, and her father. There was no doubt that she was telling the truth. She said she had her two nieces with her, and they really wanted to go home.

I said, "I have a truck." She looked surprised. I told her that she and her nieces could come with us back to Sighet. Hanolo was excited and overjoyed.

Now, I needed to convince the man who was driving the truck to take on three more passengers. I went to him, determined to get Hanolo and her two nieces on our truck. He complained, saying the truck would be too overloaded. And I told him to not worry about it, that everything would be fine, that he should be grateful that he had a truck. He glared at me for a moment and reluctantly gave in.

I found from one of the girls on our trip that the letter given to the driver by the Russian captain not only gave him safe passage but contained an additional deal. He would drive us, and in return, he could keep his truck. The Communists were planning on seizing all personal property, but he would be allowed to keep his truck with the letter the captain gave to him. I think the man realized his good fortune in getting such a deal. He would return home as the only man in town with a truck.

The miles passed with conversation and food. It might have been two days before we came to a town with an operating train. We thanked our truck driver and waved good-bye. I think that the Czech gentleman had been drinking a little potato vodka from a flask, and I believe he might have even smiled.

We were all allowed to board the train with no money, as there was none to give. I was on my last leg home and found a seat by the window. As we traveled even farther away from Auschwitz, I could feel its power over me start to release from my body. The scenery was becoming more familiar. Even though I had never been through here before, the countryside, the types of trees, the farmland, and the houses all resembled Sighet. There's no place like it in the world. I can't remember who was sitting next to me on the train as my mind drifted in and out of the present. I wondered if I would ever see Hedy and Rose or my brothers ever again. There were ten children in my family. I only knew for sure that my mother, father, my sister Ancy, and brother Mortho were gone. Part of me was afraid to find out what had happened to the rest of them. There was no safety for Jews with the Nazis. I wondered how much family I had left, if any.

Finally, we arrived in Sighet, and I stepped off of the train. I couldn't believe I was truly home again, and the relief I felt is impossible to put into words. My Auschwitz nightmare was finally over. I said my good-byes to Hanolo and to her two nieces, and we parted ways. Elie Wiesel's house was being used as a sanctuary for a lot of young people returning home, and I was invited to stay there for as long as I needed. Our families were neighbors and friends, and I was so grateful to stay at their house. I thought it would be the best way to regroup and unite myself back with the community. Maybe there I could find my family. Elie Wiesel's sister Beatrice had survived the war and camps also; she arrived home just a few weeks after me. Beatrice and I became lifelong friends and lived together on and off in the Wiesel home.

A few days after I was home, I walked through the streets of Sighet. Nothing was the same, especially me. The SS and the German soldiers were all gone, and Klara, the innocent teenage girl, was gone with them. I had changed, and so had Sighet. Our family business and all the Jewish businesses had been looted and destroyed. Windows were broken, and stores were burned inside and out. Our synagogues had been destroyed. The fence that had been constructed that sur-rounded the ghetto was no longer there. The street that the soldiers had marched us down to the deportation trains was full of activity with people recovering from the war. I was ex-hausted but surprisingly felt a new strength and steadiness from deep within. I would get to live but wouldn't know what that would truly mean for me and other survivors for some time. Every day that passed, I held on to hope that I would hear some good news about my family.

I stood alone in front of the only home I knew. Most of the windows were broken. I approached the front door with some reservation. I gently knocked and waited. After a few moments, a middle-aged Romanian woman opened the door. I told her my name was Klara Iutkovits and this was my family's home. She told me to come in. She explained that she had been stay-ing there, in the house, in the living room, for just a while. The woman seemed to be very nice. As I wandered through the rooms, she followed me, and I could feel her concern.

The rooms were cold and mostly empty. There were pa-pers scattered everywhere. I looked into my father's old of-fice. Near the baseboards was a secret place under one of the floorboards. There, my father had hidden our family pictures before our deportation. I lifted one of the boards, and there was a small satchel. I was so excited. I knew the pictures were in there, right where he had hidden them. I would be able to see my family again.

As I held the pictures in my hand, their faces looked back at me, and memories flooded my mind. I saw the faces of all of my family. My mother, my father, Joseph, Lazar, Hedy, Rose, they were all there. Again, I knew my mother, my father, and my little brother and sister were dead, but the question of who had survived was still there.

My brother Mendal had arrived with us at Auschwitz, but once we were separated, we never heard from him again. What about Joseph, Lazar, and Haskell? They weren't with us when we were deported to Auschwitz. I'm sure Hedy and Rose, if they were alive, thought I was dead. They had witnessed Dr. Mengele selecting me to go to the gas chambers. I put my head into my hands and cried. *I am healthy enough to cry again*, I thought. I had no idea when I would see any of their faces again. I realized that I had placed my entire future on the idea that my sisters would be there when I got home. I explained to the woman staying in our home that I was also looking for four silver candelabras to sell. During the ghetto and before our deportation, we had hidden them beneath the sink, in the wastewater collection tub.

I needed money to live, but when the woman and I looked for them, they were gone. She could see my disappointment and wanted to help me, but she was living day to day herself just to survive. I didn't know it, but the Romanian woman living in our house was a spiritual medium. As a matter of fact, I really didn't even know what a medium was at the time.

She took me into the kitchen, where she placed some flour on the counter and covered it with a drinking glass. She said a few words I couldn't understand. Then, before my very eyes, the flour began to move and took on the shape of a man.

I was bewildered. I didn't know what to say. The whole thing was so strange and completely effortless.

She looked at me and said, "You have one brother alive."

Well, as you would guess, I thought she was crazy, but silently in my heart, I hoped that she wasn't. I did see the flour move, and move into the shape of a man. And I have to admit, it did leave me with some hope. I decided there was nothing left for me here besides an empty house with broken windows and shattered dreams. It would have been too painful to stay there without my family. I thought that at least one of my brothers or sisters would have made it back before me. There were ten of us. With that, I said good-bye and left with my family pictures.

Maybe it was my brother Joseph's business sense rubbing off on me, or maybe it was my visit to our home that made up my mind. I became more determined than ever to find what was left of my family and resolve my financial situation. My experience at Auschwitz had left me with a strong loyalty and a belief in myself that I could overcome any difficulty. Number A-7845 had died, written down in Dr. Mengele's book of death, but Klara Iutkovits was alive.

I decided it was time to take this opportunity to rectify a financial wrong that had been done to my family during the ghetto. On my train ride back home, I had recalled a matter that was corrupt and dishonest. It had occurred to our family business during the ghetto. Our family business supplied cooking oil for the whole province, and the oil was stored in large barrels in our store cellar. My brother

Joseph, who traveled a lot, had arranged with my mother to import barrels of oil from Ireland, which had become very profitable for us. The parents of a Hungarian judge were taking advantage of the Jewish businesses that were being persecuted. They used their son as legal authority to steal from Jewish businesses. After the keys to our business were confiscated by the Hungarian gendarmes, they decided they wanted our barrels of oil because they were worth a lot of money since oil was scarce. Their son, the judge, signed an order for his parents stating that they were going to just borrow the barrels of oil. Of course, we couldn't do anything about it—we had no recourse. We knew from experience that once the barrels were gone, they were gone for good. They knew people were in grave danger, and they took advantage of the situation. It was a legal way of stealing. It was also their way of winning the approval of the Nazis and their anti-Semitism.

I was determined to find out what had happened to our barrels of oil. After the war ended, a new police headquarters was set up in Sighet. A lot of Jewish men began working there, and they had influence. I learned that the police captain was a friend of one of my brothers. His name was Ori.

I went to see him and said, "Ori, listen. Let me tell you a story." I told Ori about the barrels of oil that had been stolen from our family during the ghetto. I told him I knew the family who had taken the barrels and believed they might still have them. I asked Ori if he could help me locate our property. He agreed to help.

Ori knew the name of the people and found out where they lived. They lived in a villa in a very wealthy part of town.

Armed with Ori and the authorities to look for the barrels, when we arrived, a couple answered the door, and I recognized them right away. Although I think they knew who I was, Ori spoke and got straight to the point.

He asked, "Where did you put the barrels of oil that you took from this family, the Iutkovits?"

They looked shocked. Their past had just caught up with them, and we saw it on their faces.

They denied it. "What barrels? What are you talking about?"

Ori said, "I have a document here that gives me authority to look in your home for this family's property. Tell me where the barrels are, or I'm going to look in your house. If I find the barrels, you're in trouble, so you better tell me where they are."

I could see they were very scared and embarrassed. Finally they confessed. They said yes, they had the barrels, but there was no more oil in them. The barrels were being kept in the basement.

I knew there was no immediate use for the oil inside the barrels. The Russian army was taking everything they could put their hands on; they even took our cows. Everything had been sent back to the Russian people. We didn't have any of the simplest basic supplies, things like bread, milk, and other regular grocery items. That would take some time to be reestablished. No one could really use the oil.

Although the barrels were empty, I knew the barrels themselves were valuable. Having the advantage of Ori's support, the family agreed to release the barrels to me without any problems. Now I had to get them out of there as quickly as I could. I knew a man in town who owned a large truck that could handle the job. I convinced him to help me pick up the barrels. I told him I would pay him when I sold the barrels, and he agreed. When I returned to the villa, I was determined to get back from these people the property they had stolen from us over a year ago. I'm quite sure they thought the barrels were safe and that they had gotten away with their crime. And I'm also quite sure they would do it again if given the opportunity. There was no remorse, no apologies; no words were spoken, just a very uncomfortable silence. I wondered who else they had stolen from. As we loaded the barrels into the truck, the couple couldn't do anything except stand there, bewildered, and stare. They were lucky that was all that was going to happen; our people were murdered for our possessions.

Before the war, Joseph had made a purchasing deal for barrels of oil with a petroleum company in a city named Satu Mare. I wasn't sure if the company still existed. Satu Mare was at least a hundred miles away. We drove all night, and when we arrived at the address, there was literally nothing left except a flat, vacant lot.

Satu Mare is not a very large city, so in a very short period of time, we were able to find out that there was one petroleum company that sold large quantities of lamp oil and heating oil. When we arrived, the company owner met us right away as we drove through the gates. He said he was curious when he saw a strange truck and two people he had never seen before pull into the company's property. I was a skinny eighteen-year-old girl, and the man driving me was thirty-five. We weren't the typical work team he was used to.

He spoke to the driver first, and ignored me, but I quickly jumped in and said, "These are my barrels, sir."

He looked the cargo over and then asked me how much I wanted for the barrels. I knew Romanian money wasn't worth anything, so I told him I wanted American dollars. There was a brief pause, and then to my surprise, he agreed and offered $500, which I happily accepted. As he was handing me the money, he said we were lucky. If the Russians had stopped us, they would have taken everything we had. He then told us to be careful going back to Sighet.

The whole exchange took about fifteen minutes, and I had made my first business transaction and also restored some of my family's honor. In those days, $500 was a lot of money and I had just made myself a very rich girl. I paid the driver handsomely, and then we headed back home.

THE SEARCH BEGINS

I had enough money to last for a while, and I hoped having this money would give me enough time to find out what had happened to my family. I decided to start with my oldest brother, Joseph. I had been told that a man named Hoover, who was a city councilman, was in the munitions corps with Joseph. I went to the city council and found Mr. Hoover. I introduced myself.

I said, "Mr. Hoover, my name is Klara Iutkovits. I understand you knew my older brother. I'm looking for Joseph Iutkovits. I was told he was with you in the munitions corps. Is that true? Did you ever see him?"

He replied, "Yes, I was with your brother Joseph there."

I said "Really?" I got very excited and happy.

And he said, "Unfortunately, they killed him. They shot him in the head. I can't even remember what reason they gave or if they even gave a reason. I'm so sorry. It was horrible." His face was still pleasant and sympathetic as I walked away.

I don't remember what happened after that. The only thing I can recall is that I was outside, standing on a balcony. It was nighttime.

I looked up into the sky, and I saw the stars, and I said, "God, how did you allow that? How could you let something so sad and so horrible happen?"

As I've said before, I have five brothers, but Joseph was very special to me. He was such a nice brother; he was wise like my father. My father was the spiritual leader and head of our family, and he was gone. Joseph was the brilliant mind of our family. He worked hard for our family. I never believed I would not see him again. He was my hero. I cried so much that night and thought, *Now he's gone, too.*

And now, it has been so many years that there are no more tears left to cry for my mother, for my father, for my sisters, for my brothers who were killed. But I guess some people are cruel, and some people are good. And that's the core of every nation. There's good and bad. Even among the Germans, there are good people and bad people.

A few weeks had gone by since I'd heard the news of my brother Joseph, and I was home alone when there was a knock at the door. I opened the door, and a German soldier in a disheveled uniform was standing outside the doorway. I was immediately taken aback with disbelief.

He wasn't wearing the black SS uniform that I was used to seeing at Auschwitz. His uniform was the standard green and gray. He looked very dirty and unkempt and had come from a prison camp for German soldiers. The German prisoners were required to go through a detainment process before they were allowed to go back home to Germany. Once they were released, they were on their own, like everyone else.

As we stood there in silence, looking at each other, he finally spoke and said, "Haben Sie etwas zu essen geben? Ich bin hungrig. Könnten Sie mir etwas zu essen?" This means, "Do you have something to eat? I'm hungry. Could you give me some food?"

I most likely took a very long time to answer, it was the first time I had seen a German soldier since Auschwitz. I remember I thought to myself, *Maybe he killed my brother, or my mother, or my father.* And then I thought, *The war is over, and standing in front me is that living proof.* Proof showing me that it was truly over. No newspaper headlines or radio broadcast, just a surrendered, broken man in a dirty uniform, and me, raw humanity. And my heart began to move me. I thought, *I'm going to give him something to eat.*

I said, "Sie warten hier," which means, "You wait here." I went and got him some food. I'm not sure what it was, but I brought it to him.

He paused and said, "Danke schön! Danke schön!" ("Thank you! Thank you!") and slowly walked away.

I grew up in a very loving and very charitable family. This was my experience. This is what they would have wanted me to do; my heart said it was the right thing for me. Although it was a spontaneous gesture, it was symbolic in nature. It

grounded me firmly in the belief that just because all conditions might be right for me to do harm, like what was done to
us, I wasn't going to throw out the lessons and love I had experienced as a child. To me, that would have been dishonor-
ing my mother and father, their life, and the people they were.

GOING TO PRAGUE

As I had mentioned earlier, I was staying at Elie Wiesel's home, and his sister Beatrice and I had become very close friends. Beatrice wanted to go to Prague and help me search for Hedy and Rose. Some weeks had gone by, and there had been absolutely no word from either of them.

She said, "Klara, there is nothing here for us right now, and we should go." We had heard of other families reuniting in Prague, so I agreed.

Beatrice had found some gold and silver that her family had hidden. So as soon as we could, we made arrangements to leave for Prague. The opportunity to go and search for Hedy and Rose provided me with a strong purpose. I was so excited when we boarded the train. It carried so many people, people from all walks of life. Right away, I noticed new postwar energy on the faces of most of the people I looked at. I felt an optimism that I hadn't felt before. I knew that my sisters' story may well end like most stories ended after the war, but I was still very hopeful. I had to try to find them. I knew if anyone could survive, it would be Hedy and Rose. Two missing girls in a country of missing people would hardly be missed. But they were the two most important people in my world, and I had no idea if they had made it out of Auschwitz. I made sure I brought our family pictures that I had recently found.

There was still a good deal of postwar danger and lawless-ness across Europe. Europe was confused and had a sense of anarchy about it as it picked itself up from the ashes. Rogue Russian soldiers didn't help. I had heard and knew of plenty of horror stories. They were always armed and hovered about doing as they pleased. When we boarded the train to Prague, there were quite a few Russian soldiers spread out through the train in little packs. We did our best to avoid and ignore them. Sighet, and most of Eastern Europe, was now in the hands of Stalin and the Russian authority.

I think it was when we were somewhere near Prague that I looked up as a Russian soldier was walking toward us. We knew he was coming over to us because he never took his eyes off of us. His friends grinned as they watched him. I hoped for the best but could feel Beatrice's anxiety as he came closer. We had no idea what he could want, and there was nothing we could do anyway.

When he got to us, he leaned over and said, "Give me your purses."

We had hidden most of our money in our shoes and had kept a small amount in our purses. But I had put all my family pictures that I had found in my purse. We had no choice but to hand them over.

I gave the soldier my purse. I said, "I have my family pictures in there. Can I keep them?"

He didn't say anything. He just scowled and walked away with our property and moved on to the next car. I was devastated. Nobody was going to stop or arrest a Russian soldier for anything. Those pictures were all I had left, and now I had just lost all of them; family pictures, letters, and papers, everything gone just that quick. Now what would I do?

Prague is one of the most stunning cities in the world. Although it had been bombed, most of Prague's infrastructure was preserved. I found the city breathtaking when I visited it the first time. Prague is so rich with ancient cathedral-style buildings designed in historical architecture.

The old city square was full of bright colors, charming cafés, shops, restaurants, and other businesses. There were different places where you could go and look down on the city and see all these magnificent red rooftops. Prague was so much fun, so engaging, and in some ways, it was a fairy-tale experience for us. When Beatrice and I walked at night along the winding cobblestone streets, I was always fascinated by the old gas lamp street posts. They produced a low, warm amber glow that barely lit the streets at all.

Beatrice and I shared a room at the Imperial Hotel in Prague. Our favorite place to go to was the Café Arco, and it quickly became a dependable meeting place. There at the café, a lot of young people would spend time together enjoying the company of friends and would discuss the war and all of the latest subject matter of the time. It was also a place where lots of problems were solved. People found jobs, solved money problems, lodging issues were resolved, people fell in love, but more importantly, people discovered information about loved ones who were separated because of the war. Sometimes, the information was good, and other times, it was bad. For the people whose loved ones were reunited, it was a celebrated occasion. For those who received bad news about their loved ones, there was closure, but it was always a sad time.

Traveling through Prague was one of the very limited ways that people could make it back to their homes because most of the railroads were bombed out. Other approaches could be very dangerous. Jews came through Prague from camps like Terezín, Treblinka, Sobibor, Mauthausen, and Auschwitz.

Our stay in Prague was where we began to really discover the enormity of the Nazi atrocities. We came across numerous Czechoslovakian Jews who had arrived back home to Prague from the different camps. They weren't at all energetic and youthful like Beatrice and me. Some were children; some were old, injured, and lost, with nobody left from their families to help them. Starting from scratch, they would have to go through the same thing that I had gone though in Sighet. Somehow, alone with nothing, they had to try to put their lives back together again. Although we were just a little farther ahead of them in some areas, we were still on that path.

With my support, I had a little more time to adjust and settle in; that was the only actual difference. Restarting their lives would be very difficult, and they would each come to grips with it differently.

Every day when the train stopped at the Prague train station, Beatrice and I looked to see if Hedy and Rose were on it...They never were. Other people searched, too. I saw people reunite with their families all the time. Beatrice already knew that her brother and sister were okay and staying in Paris. She was predominately there to give me strength and to help me as a friend. Beatrice was a very bright girl; she helped keep me from being discouraged several times when I would feel more than a little frustrated.

We had been there a couple of months with no word from Hedy or Rose. Then, one day, I was called to the front desk. There was a letter for me. A few weeks before I came to Prague, I briefly ran into a woman from Sighet named Yolan. She used to work very hard for our family business, shelling nuts, and she recognized me. Immediately, she reintroduced herself. We talked with each other for a little while. We caught up on our lives, and then I mentioned to her I was going to Prague. That was all. We said our good-byes, and we went our separate ways.

One day, Yolan was walking in downtown Sighet, and she thought she saw me again. She approached the girl, thinking it was me, and said, "Hi, Klara."

The girl said, "I'm sorry. I'm not Klara. I'm Klara's sister Hedy. Unfortunately, Klara was killed at Auschwitz."

Yolan then said, "No, no! You look so much like Klara. Klara's alive! She was just here. She's alive. I saw her! She went to Prague."

The letter I held in my hand was from Hedy and Rose, telling me they were alive and that they wanted me to come back home. In their letter, they wrote that they were staying at Elie Wiesel's home.

Beatrice and I jumped up and down screaming with joy, "They're alive! They're alive! Hedy and Rose are alive!" We were elated and baffled at the same time. They had to have come through Prague. How did we miss them?

And then I remembered we had missed one day going to the train station the whole time we were in Prague. Could that have been the day? It must have been. I was truly perplexed, after giving all of my best efforts, searching high and low in Prague for them for months. One more time, divinity stepped in and assisted me, making it possible for my heart's desire to be reconnected with what I could not do on my own, find and reconnect with my two sisters, Hedy and Rose.

Beatrice had not lost any of her enthusiasm supporting me, but she wanted to go on to Paris to meet up with her younger brother, Elie. So we said our good-byes and made a promise to each other that we would meet back up in a few months.

A WHOLE NEW CHAPTER

Right before I left Prague, I met a girl named Toby, from Sighet. We became friendly and enjoyed quite a few conversations together at the Café Arco. Toby had heard the news that I found my sisters alive and that I was returning to Sighet. Mail service wasn't very reliable after the war, and most forms of communication were very limited. Friends, family, acquaintances, and sometimes complete strangers would help with delivering letters and other items, depending upon the circumstances. It was a very important part of the postwar effort because it seemed like everybody was looking for somebody. After she congratulated me on finding my sisters, she wanted to know if I could deliver a letter for her to a young gentleman named Ezra. Her request was that I find Ezra, deliver the letter to him, and ask him if he would give the letter to his brother. Even though Toby never told me why, I could tell she liked this man very much. I told her that I would.

This time, the train ride back home to Sighet was unbelievably special. I was on my way back home to be reunited with family. For the first time since Auschwitz, I could feel the emotional celebration rushing through my whole body. Everything glowed. The world seemed brighter and more alive. Of course, the passengers didn't know, but I felt like all of the people on board the train knew about my journey and were all going home with me. Hedy and Rose had no idea that I was on my way back to Sighet or if I had even gotten their letter. Contacting them by phone was impossible. When I arrived, I expected a great reunion. I had hoped to surprise Hedy and Rose and went directly to Beatrice's home, but when I arrived, my sisters weren't there.

I found out I had just missed them by one day. They had decided to leave and visit our cousins in a city not far from Sighet, called Cluj. Well, as you can imagine, I was quite disappointed, but at this point, it was just another hurdle to jump over, and I had grown accustomed to that. I also felt secure in the fact that they were with my cousins, and now it was just a matter of getting to Cluj.

Before I left for Cluj, I remembered the letter Toby had given me. I didn't have time to look up Ezra and deliver it before I had to leave, yet I knew how important it was to her, especially after my own experience, and didn't want to let her down. Therefore, I recruited one of the girls who was staying with us at the house to help me. I needed to leave Sighet with a clear conscience. I gave her the same instructions that Toby gave me, and she assured me she would deliver the letter. The conditions in Sighet were starting to improve more rapidly, and a few buses were running short distances outside of town. The bus station in Sighet is located beside the train station, and you can walk to it in just a few minutes from anywhere in town. At that time, no trains were going to Cluj, so the bus was the only way to get there. After I took care of the matter of the letter, I got the address of my cousins from a friend, and I gathered a few things and jumped on a bus bound for Cluj. The ride was about 120 miles, or about a half a day. I had never been to Cluj, and when I arrived in town, it was just getting dark. I was given directions at the bus station and was told my cousins' home was not far away and that I could walk if I wanted to, so off I went.

I knew in my heart this was finally it! I don't know how I knew it, but I just did. Hedy and Rose would be there, but they had no idea I was coming. I could feel a unity and a new beginning start to happen even before I got there. I was finally at the end of my journey. I'm not sure what time it was or how long I had been walking when I got to my cousins', but the lights were all on. It was all a blur from there. I can't even remember who answered the door, but as you can imagine, we had an unbelievable reunion. We were crying, laughing, and screaming; it was a party. We had survived and were all happy, healthy, and beautiful and had the rest of our lives before us. We cooked and ate a delicious meal. Not one word was spoken about Auschwitz that night; there would be plenty of time for that. At that moment, we simply enjoyed each other and celebrated the good news in our lives.

Klara's only two sisters that survived Auschwitz. Rose on the left and Hedy on the right.

Cluj was quite different from Prague but still an amazingly beautiful city. It's more modern today, but back then, the architecture in Cluj was very old-world and had a Gothic Renaissance atmosphere. We enjoyed exploring the city when we were able to. Sometimes, we would go to the cinema, or shop, or eat at the different cafés. But mostly, we spent a lot of time just being together while we caught up and made our different plans for the future. Hedy and Rose had visited our old house when they first returned to Sighet. They had found our home in the same state that I did, except the woman staying there was gone. We decided to sell the house when we got back.

I was so excited because Rose had become engaged to be married before she came to Cluj. She planned to have her wedding in Sighet. Her fiancé was a very lucky man; Rose was gracious and very beautiful. She was forever looking out for me and guiding me and had a special loving tone in her voice when she called me by my name. It felt exclusive for me, as though Rose was my guardian angel. I loved her so much.

After four or five amazing weeks together, we returned to Sighet. I was very happy to go back with Rose and Hedy. For my sisters and me, Rose's wedding would become the first strong symbol that would continue us on toward our lives of freedom.

We found a gentleman who owned a shoemaking business who was interested in the purchase of our old house. He offered us $200 and said he would make us new pairs of beautiful boots. It doesn't seem like a lot now, but it wasn't bad for the times and circumstances. We all agreed to the offer. For me, that was a very emotional day, and I really just kept to myself. I had so many fond memories attached to that house. What made it a home for me, though, were my mother and father. Without them, it was just another building.

Rose, Hedy, and I were, again, staying with the others at Elie Wiesel's house. While Rose busily planned her wedding, I discovered that the letter Toby had given me in Prague was never delivered. For some reason, the girl I had given the letter to could never locate Ezra. I felt terrible for Toby. I had made her a promise. The next day, I took the letter back and placed it on the dresser. I decided to go into town and ask around to see if anybody knew this Ezra.

After I'd been walking for some time and had asked several people if they knew him, I stepped into one of the local shops. I asked the owner if he knew of a man named Ezra. I said, "He's about twenty-six years old and in the cattle business. I have a letter for him."

The shop owner said, "You're in luck; as a matter of fact, I do know him. He just walked by. He shouldn't be far." We walked outside, and he spotted Ezra right away and pointed him out to me. He said, "That's him. That's Ezra right over there."

I quickly caught up with him and said, "Hi, my name is Klara. I have a letter for you from Prague to give to your brother."

He seemed surprised and said, "Sure, fine," and waited for me to give him the letter.

I smiled and said, "Oh, I don't have it with me. You'll have come back with me to where I'm staying to get the letter. It's not far. Would that be possible?"

He said he was in Sighet on business, but since it was not that far, he would come with me to get it. On the way, we talked very little, but he told me his name was Ezra Wizel.

I said, "I know." I could tell he liked me. When we got back to the house, I couldn't find the letter. I looked everywhere. I was so embarrassed. I must have misplaced it somewhere. We agreed that he would come back to get it later that night.

Finally, I found the letter behind the small dresser that I had put it on. When Ezra returned that night, I had it waiting for him. He seemed different, much more relaxed and not so much in a hurry. I gave the letter to Ezra, which he didn't seem to have the slightest interest in. He was interested in me. He wanted to know if I would like to go on a date with him. He wouldn't tell me where because he wanted it to be a surprise. I was a little reluctant but decided I would go anyway. We made plans for the following Saturday.

When Ezra came to take me on our date that Saturday, we had to walk because of Shabbat. The walk was pleasant and cheerful, and when we finally arrived at our destination, a big, beautiful cherry orchard spread out before us. The trees were thick with green leaves and filled with ripe cherries.

Ezra said, "Surprise! We are going to have a picnic." He took me to a very nice part of the orchard where everything was already laid out and arranged. Ezra was very good friends with the man who ran the cherry orchard, who brought us a wicker basket stuffed with fresh, delicious red cherries. When we ran out, Ezra's friend would bring us another fresh bunch of cherries.

We ate lots of cherries that day, and we talked for hours about everything. Ezra said this orchard reminded him of the area he grew up in the Maramures Province. Being that we were both Jewish we had everything in common. We talked about our families and when we were young. Ezra told me that he was never deported to a concentration camp but remained a soldier without arms during the war until the liberation. He also said how happy he was to be reunited with his sister and two brothers who had been imprisoned.

Later he told me that the letter I had given him for his brother, from Toby, was a sweet letter, but he didn't think his brother was very interested in her.

Ezra was a true gentleman, and as nighttime approached, he told me, "We better start walking back before it gets too late." As we left, he turned to me and said he had one surprise left for me.

When we got to the gate of the cherry orchard, I saw a horse and buggy approaching. I said, "Oh my! Is this for us?"

A man, who owned the horse and buggy and worked for Ezra, had come to give us a ride back into town. I couldn't help but feel how fortunate I was to be alive in that moment, riding back home in a horse and buggy with Ezra. It was a beautifully clear night, and every star in the universe seemed to be out.

I smiled as I thought to myself, *I guess that no one else but me was supposed to deliver that letter.*

THE WORLD GETS BIGGER

At that time in Sighet, we quickly found out that our freedom, unfortunately, would be short-lived if we were to stay in Eastern Europe. Leaving Europe was something that Hedy and Rose and I had seriously talked about after being reunited in Cluj. We didn't understand—as most people didn't understand—Stalin and Communism, but what we did know is that the Communists were rapidly closing borders and restricting travel. This, to us, was all too familiar. Sighet was back in Romanian hands but was occupied by Stalin and his Russian troops. The Russians installed a pro-Soviet government that sealed our borders and made it illegal to travel to other countries. It would, in fact, be very difficult for all of us to leave Romania.

Opportunity came for us when the Canadian government instituted anti-discrimination laws and eased immigration regulations. The Canadian Jewish community was working tirelessly to bring displaced persons to Canada. They introduced an adoption program, but the process could take as long as two years. Between 1941 and 1951, thousands of Jews were allowed to emigrate from Europe to Canada.

Hedy's window of opportunity to flee Romania and the Communist regime came at the same time Rose was to be married. It was a difficult decision for all of us, but we had learned through experience not to procrastinate when it came to our freedom. Hedy's chance came first when a family in Canada agreed to adopt her and take her in. She would need to travel from Romania to Hungary before she could move about unrestricted. Although we were all so excited for her, we knew how dangerous this would be. If she made it to Hungary safely without being picked up by the authorities, she could travel to Germany and then go through the process of getting to Canada, but she would have to act quickly.

Beatrice was still residing in Paris and wanted to leave Europe as well. It would have been much easier for her to leave Europe through Paris; after all, she was now free from the authoritarian regimes, and all she had to do was go through the emigration process. However, she was such a good friend, and so very close to Hedy, she decided to risk her freedom and return to Sighet in order to help her get out of Romania. Her courage and selfless act of friendship is something that I always admired and will never forget. Our days were yet again filled with danger and uncertainty. Precisely the way the Nazis had occupied our land and destroyed anything free and good, Stalin and the Russian Communists were having their turn.

Hedy and Beatrice packed very little that day. We were crying and hugging as we said our good-byes. I felt so sad and empty watching them as they left. Beatrice was very experienced in traveling throughout Europe, so I knew Hedy was in good hands. They both would be doing a lot of walking, and would have to vigilantly make their way to the Romanian-Hungarian border, which could be very dangerous. If you were stopped, you would be interrogated and could be arrested and detained indefinitely. Many people who were caught were never seen again.

Beatrice knew that once they got to the border, they could meet up with people from different underground groups, people who could help them get past the Russian military and slip over the border into Hungary. As I said, Hungary was more open and uncontrolled, which made it easier to move about. From there, you could travel without the authoritarian restrictions. Ironically, Germany would become the key for Hedy and Beatrice and others to immigrate into Canada from Sighet. Of course, Rose and I would be busy with wedding plans, but we would still worry until we received word that they were safe in Germany.

Rose's wedding was beautiful. I was so happy for her. Her wedding was a traditional Jewish wedding, and the ceremony was held at Elie Wiesel's house. Rose seemed so happy and was such a beautiful bride. Hedy and Beatrice were truly missed, and after some weeks, we finally received word that they had made it safely to Germany. The good news was that they made it to Germany. The bad news was that they had discovered that making it to Canada from Germany would take much longer than they had anticipated. It wasn't a simple process. Getting all their paperwork to leave Germany was, in itself, an enormous bureaucratic undertaking.

About a year after Hedy and Beatrice left, Rose and her husband were forced to leave Sighet. Rose's husband, Allen, owned a small deli near the train station in Sighet. The Communist government had made it illegal to own private businesses and was threatening to arrest Rose's husband and take away his business. Allen had family in the United States who could help them immigrate if they could make it to Germany. They decided it was best to leave Sighet as soon as possible. Taking the same route as Hedy and Beatrice, Rose and Allen made it to Germany. They met up with Hedy and Beatrice, who were still waiting for their immigration paperwork to go through. Eventually, Rose and Allen immigrated safely to the United States. It took some time for Hedy and Beatrice to make it to Canada, but their day finally came, and off they went to start their new lives there.

Ezra Wizel and I were married December 10, 1947. I was twenty years old, and Ezra was twenty-six. It was a very small wedding, with maybe forty or fifty people in attendance. Even though I was getting married and should have been happy, I was very sad. I remember it was a horribly rainy day. I looked around at all of the guests after the ceremony, and there was not a soul from my family there. Nobody, not my sisters, my brothers, my mother, or father were at our wedding. Hedy and Rose were gone. We had been through so much together, and of course I was happy for them, but I really needed my older sisters to support me.

The absence of my family was very sad and overwhelming. The rabbi could see I was sad and tried to cheer me up, saying, "Klara, if your parents were alive, what a big, beautiful wedding you would have had."

I went into the other room by myself, and I started crying, and I just couldn't stop.

When Ezra found me, he said, "Klara, why are you crying? Don't worry. I'm going to be good to you."

I cried, "It's not you. It's not you." I cried so much it felt like somebody had just died. I couldn't stop because it was such a sad thing for me to be there getting married with nobody from my family there.

Ezra and I spent the next three years living in Sighet, which was becoming more difficult because of Communist rule. Ezra continued to work buying and selling cattle from surrounding farms in other towns, but the government was clamping down on privately owned businesses. You could be arrested for no reason. Other people disappeared, and we'd never see them again. Ezra and I were growing more and more concerned with Stalin's anti-Jewish emigration policies. Jews were not allowed to emigrate, and we felt trapped. Relief came when Ana Pauker, who was head of the Communist Party in Romania, became prime minister and decided she would oppose the law. In 1950, she created a law that allowed Jews to immigrate to Israel.

In 1951, Ezra and I got our passports and left Sighet, Romania, forever. The country and home that I grew up in and that I was so fond of as a little girl had been destroyed by the Hitler and Stalin regimes. Not only had the country changed—I had changed. I was no longer a little girl. Most of my family was gone, and there was nothing to keep me in Sighet. I was twenty-four years old, and it was time for me to start a new life with Ezra somewhere else. We just knew that going to Israel would give us a fresh start.

In Israel, we found a place to live and work at a kibbutz, which in Hebrew means "a communal settlement." The kibbutz was set up by the Israeli government. We received room and board, and in exchange, we were required to work. Ezra had a job working with the agriculture, and I worked in the dining room that served all of the people that lived and worked there. Along with the room and board, we received a small income. But mostly, it was great to be liberated from the worries of war and anti-Semitism.

In 1952, after about a year in Israel, Ezra and I entered a program that would take us to Canada. We were grateful for everything that had been done for us in Israel, but Ezra felt he could do very well in the cattle business in Canada. We could also be reunited with Hedy, Beatrice, and my cousin, who would be there to help us. We made all of the necessary arrangements to leave Israel. To get to Canada, first, we had to travel by ship for one week to London, England, with a group of fellow emigrants. I was very excited to find out that we would have to first stop in London. There we would have to report to the Canadian Embassy. Once we arrived in London, we were taken to a school, where we stayed in the dormitory. It was nice, and to me, it was like a hotel.

After a few days, Ezra and I reported to the Canadian Embassy. I couldn't speak a word of English, so I had no idea what anyone was talking about, and it caused me to laugh a lot. My laughing seemed to have broken the ice and made them like us. I don't know why, but it seemed like the more I laughed, the more it seemed like they wanted to help us. We were assigned a translator who told us that the process could take about two months. And one of the women who worked at the embassy, who really liked us, said she would help to try to speed up the process of our papers. Ezra and I were expecting to be in London for a while, so we had fun walking around and sight-seeing. We were very surprised to hear, after only about four days, that we were going to Canada!

When we arrived in Canada, we stayed with Beatrice until we got our own apartment. Hedy had gone to California to visit Rose, who was having a baby. She was able to stay with Rose for one year, until her visa expired.

Now that we were in Canada, speaking English was more important than ever. I listened to the radio every day. My favorite song was a hit by Patti Page called "You Belong to Me." I would sing the song over and over again until I had the words memorized. I didn't know what the words meant, so I asked Beatrice to explain them to me. To also help with my English, I went to the movies, sometimes twice a week, even though it was expensive. And before I knew it, Ezra and I were having conversations in English.

Klara and Ezra Wizel

During the fourteen years we lived in Canada, Ezra became very successful in the meat industry, and we had two wonderful daughters, Freya and Judy.

Klara and Ezra with daughter Freya

Klara with daughters, Judy and Freya

EPILOGUE

Over time, and through some great networking from friends and Jewish organizations, we were able to put together as best we could what had happened to the rest of my family. My brothers Joseph and Haskell were in the Hungarian military, where Joseph was shot and killed. In actuality, it was no military at all. It was just Nazi slave labor. We found out during the war that my brother Haskell had made his way back to Sighet from the military. For what reasons, I'm not sure. He was arrested in Sighet, then deported to Auschwitz sometime after our deportation. I don't know if he ever met up with my brother Mendal, who was separated from us the night we all arrived at Auschwitz.

During our initial selection process, I knew my brother Mendal was not selected or killed. My sisters and I tried continuously to find out how he was and what his condition was while we were still in Auschwitz, but we couldn't get any information. It was impossible.

What I did find out is that neither one of them survived. Sometimes, I think about Haskell and Mendal, and I pray that they got to see each other again. Both Haskell and Mendal loved sports. If I close my eyes, I can still see them as the fun-loving brothers they were, playing soccer or snow skiing. It makes me feel better that God might have made it possible for them to have been together before they died.

We also discovered my oldest sister, Ety, who had come on the last transport from Sighet to Auschwitz, died at the Mauthausen concentration camp. Mauthausen's policy was to work the prisoners to death. Each time we learned news of my family, I felt the hurt and sadness all over again, and it took me a quite a while to recover.

The only family member we could not account for was my brother Lazar. And no one seemed to know what happened to him at all. It wasn't until one day about twenty years later, after Ezra and I had relocated to Westwood, California, to be close to Rose, that I got a phone call. My brother Lazar had been located by one of my cousins. I couldn't believe it! He was alive and had been living in Russia all this time! I couldn't help but think about the old woman I found living in our house in Sighet after the war. She had taken flour and sprinkled it on the kitchen counter and placed a glass over the flour. The flour moved into the shape of a man. And that was when she told me that I had one brother alive. And then, twenty years later, we found out that she was right; one brother, Lazar, had survived. I can't explain it. I'm only telling you what happened. After contacting him and submitting the necessary paperwork, Lazar was able to fly to Canada to live with Hedy, and then later he came to live in California.

Klara and siblings from left to right. Hedy, Klara, Lazar and Rose

Klara and siblings from left to right. Hedy, Lazar, Rose and Klara

All in all, after what I went through, I feel like a very, very lucky lady. Unfortunately, the sad thing about it is that my family didn't come back. If my family would have come back, it would have been much easier to move on. The hurt is there in their place. To be surrounded by such a nice, good family and to have it taken away is the worst thing there is. But what I can say is this: Life must go on, and try your best. And I still have to say, thank God for every day.

One time, back in Sighet, not too long after the war, I dreamed that my father came to me. I said to him, "Thank God you're here! I'm so lonely. I don't want to be here. I feel dead alone. I want to go with you."

He smiled to comfort me and said, "No, Klara, you're not coming with me."

I said, "Yes, I am. I don't want to stay here. I don't want to be alone, and I'm going to go with you."

Again he said, "Absolutely not, you must stay...You're not coming with me."

It's amazing, but it's a true story. I saw him flying up to the heavens. It was so strange that I dreamed that! I saw him flying up. So there must be something there.

You know, one time I saw a documentary with Einstein. And they asked him, "Do you believe there is a god?"

And he answered, "I studied a lot about it. I couldn't say there is not a god, but I couldn't say there is one."

And I say it's a beautiful thing to believe—to believe in God. Even though there are some people that don't, I believe God is everywhere. It's a beautiful feeling to believe in something. Where would you be if you didn't believe? Look what happened to me as a young girl. I believe my faith is what kept me going. I guess it was meant to be that I should be alive to tell you this story here.

I shared a life with Ezra for forty-three years. He was the nicest, finest man and the best father anybody could wish for. Ezra and I had a wonderful marriage, and I still consider myself a very, very, very lucky lady.

———⟡———

Today, Klara Wizel is an inspiring and successful businesswoman living in Westwood, California. Her two daughters, Freya and Judy, and her grandchildren live close by. She is a member of The 1939 Society, nicknamed the "1939" Club, a Holocaust survivors organization, where she is active in assisting other Holocaust survivors and keeping the memory of those who died sacred. Through her experience, Klara uses the opportunity to educate humanity about genocide.

Klara Wizel

It is not known if anyone but Klara escaped Mengele after he selected them to be killed in the gas chamber at Auschwitz. What is known is that Mengele loved to kill, and Klara loved life. And for just one brief instance, for the tens of thousands Mengele put to death, Klara's love for life—and her escape— triumphed and spoke for all others who loved life, too, but were murdered.

Klara and Ezra

Ezra, Freya, Judy and Klara

Klara's sister Hedy's wedding in Canada, 1953. Nathan, Hedy and Klara

Klara's sister Hedy's wedding party

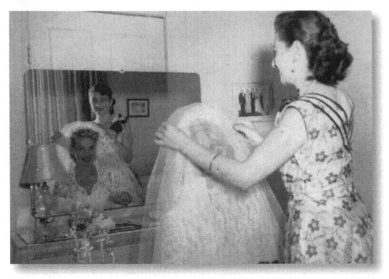

Klara adjusting Hedy's veil

Klara's sisters Rose and Hedy

Klara and daughter Freya

From left to right. Klara's daughter Freya, Klara, sisters Hedy and Rose and Klara's daughter Judy

Ezra and Klara

Klara and Rose

Klara's sister, Hedy Korman, accepting Woman of the Year award from the Jewish Society in Winnipeg presented by Rabbi Ephraim Bryks.

RABBI EPHRAIM BRYKS
84-33 116th Street
Richmond Hill, N.Y. 11418

Wednesday, April 17, 1996

It is with a deep sense of sadness and loss that I write this letter on the passing of Mrs. Hedy Korman. Professional educators without exception, have attributed a childs success or failure on the education given to them in their very early years of formal schooling. The love, devotion and warm smile given to any three year old helps to mold the mind and fashion the soul. The Sages of the Talmud compare teachers to the stars in the heavens. The commentaries explain that just as stars shine at night so too are the words we teach during the daytime reviewed and shared in the evening. And just as the stars brightness is no less diminished during the daytime (although not perceived by the human eye) so too are teachers words and guidance felt during the daytime although not always seen or noticed.

Hedy was a Pre-School childs delight and a mothers dream. A parent knew that with Hedy in the classroom their child was safe and secure. She knew from years of experience and a wonderful personality that was second nature to her the exact amount of teaching, playing, prodding and crying any child needed. An entire generation of children first experienced school under her warm smile and guiding hand.

To her loving husband, Nathan, and family I can truly say that we all join in your loss and the void left behind. Her hard work towards every Jewish cause, the hours she spent cooking and baking, making her world famous knishes, making sure every program was a huge success. Hedy had ideas and plans to raise money no one could ever imagine. To see her negotiate at the shul's annual garage sale - which she organized and ran - was sheer delight. But she always turned a profit and with it her classroom purchased another car to ride in or a toy to climb on or a puzzle to play with. In a world where we often loose sight of priorities, Hedy's were always crystal clear. Her family, her Shul, her School, the membership and the children those were hers. This is the proud legacy she leaves behind and for this she will always be fondly remembered.

Our leaders have established this week as a week of remembrance for the horrors of the past. Almighty G-d has chosen to take from us one of our shinning lights as a symbol of what one person can accomplish building for the future.

May her memory be a blessing, may her repose be of peace.

"התהא נשמתה אדא האדם אשר האדם בגן עדן"

Rabbi Ephraim Bryks

Condolence letter from Rabbi Ephraim Bryks to the family of Hedy Korman. Letter may be read in full in the back of this book.

Klara Wizel with her daughters, Freya and Judy. Award ceremony for the Cinema City International Film Festival, 2009. The Klara Wizel Story was awarded Audience Choice for Best Documentary.

Klara Wizel and Danny Naten at the AOF International Film Festival, 2009. Alan J. Bailey Excellence Awards in the category of Social Commentary chose The Klara Wizel Story as the official winner.

AFTERWORD

The day Danny met Klara will be forever imprinted in my mind. He was introduced to her by chance, by his acting manager. Danny spent several hours with Klara that first meeting, and the impact she had on him was immediately evident to me during our conversation on his way home. I knew the intensity in his voice came directly from what she had shared with him. That evening, Danny shared with me more of what Klara had told him of her family, her time spent at Auschwitz, her incredible will to live, and her miraculous escape. At times, he was speechless while gathering his thoughts, and I could tell he was extremely moved by what he had heard. Who knew this seemingly normal woman would have within her a story that so completely stirred my husband and, as he said, "put life in perspective."

Klara had never told her story publicly, and Danny was determined to have her story heard. After a few months of encouragement, Danny convinced Klara that her story should be heard, whether presented by him or by someone else. They talked frequently and met often to discuss the possibility of making a documentary of her life story. Over time they developed a friendship based on the admiration and trust they had for each other and because of this special bond, Klara chose Danny to be the vessel to make her story available to all who wanted to hear it.

Later, with help from Randy Gifford, his writing partner, myself, the typist, and Carrie Smith for her help in editing, the story came together in print form. Danny's 100 percent commitment inspired us all.

These last two years, I've been focused on Klara's story along with grieving my own most intimate loss. My husband, Danny, was taken from all of us as he passed away suddenly in December 2012. Working on this book has helped me keep the focus on the important things in life while still feeling connected with him. The lessons I've learned from both of them continue to strengthen and inspire me. I've drawn from that strength and, through it, was devoted to finishing this book for both Klara and Danny.

I'd like to end by saying this: Klara touched the hearts of all those involved in this project in ways you may never imagine, especially Danny's and mine. My hope is that this story inspires you the way it did us the first time we heard it.

Beverly Naten

Danny and Beverly Naten

AUTHOR BIOGRAPHIES

Danny Naten, actor, writer, and director was led by his passion for the arts and film to Hollywood. With acting credits in films, which include Love Hollywood Style and What Doesn't Kill You, Naten went on to write and direct the independent dark comedy Black Russian as well as the award-winning documentary Auschwitz Escape: The Klara Wizel Story. Visit www.bandanapictures.

Danny Naten

com for more about Danny Naten and view the trailer to the documentary Auschwitz Escape: The Klara Wizel Story.

R .J. Gifford culled through pages of transcripts and hours of interviews to produce the first draft of the book version of Auschwitz Escape: The Klara Wizel Story. He is honored to help bring this story to life, perhaps the only story on record of someone escaping Mengele's selection process.

Rabbi Ephraim Bryks
84-33 116th Street
Richmond Hill, N.Y. 11418

Wednesday, April 17, 1996

It is with a deep sense of sadness and loss that I write this letter on the passing of Mrs. Hedy Korman. Professional educators without exception have attributed a child's success or failure on the education given to them in their very early years of formal schooling. The love, devotion and warm smile given to any three year old helps to mold the mind and fashion the soul. The Sages of the Talmud compare teachers to the stars in the heavens. The commentaries explain that just as stars shine at night so too are the words we teach during the daytime reviewed and shared in the evening. And just as the stars brightness is no less diminished during the daytime (although not perceived by the human eye) so too are a teachers words and guidance felt during the daytime although not always seen or noticed.

Hedy was a Pre-School child's delight and a mothers dream. A parent knew that with Hedy in the classroom their child was safe and secure. She knew from years of experience and a wonderful personality that was second nature to her the exact amount of teaching, playing, prodding and crying any child needed. An entire generation of children first experienced school under her warm smile and guiding hand.

To her loving husband, Nathan, and family I can truly say that we all join in your loss and the void left behind. Her hard work towards every Jewish cause, the hours she spent cooking and baking, making her world famous knishes, making sure every program was a huge success. Hedy had ideas and plans to raise money no one could ever imagine. To see her negotiate at the shul's annual garage sale – which she organized and ran – was sheer delight. But she always turned a profit and with it her classroom purchased another car to ride in or a toy to climb on or a puzzle to play with. In a world where we often loose sight of priorities, Hedy's were always crystal clear. Her family, her shul, her school, the membership and the children those were hers. This is the proud legacy she leaves behind and for this she will always be fondly remembered.

Our leaders have established this week as a week of remembrance for the horrors of the past. Almighty G-d has chosen to take from us one of our shinning lights as a symbol of what one person can accomplish building for the future.

May her memory be a blessing, may her repose be of peace.

Rabbi Ephraim Bryks

REFERENCES

1. Telegram from Erich Ludendorff to Paul von Hindenburg after he appointed Hitler as Chancellor. Quoted in "The Holocaust: A Primary Source History" - by Judy Bartel - History – 2005

2. The Anti-Nazi Boycott of 1933, American Jewish Historical Society. Accessed January 22, 2009.